BLACK WARRANT

Sunil Gupta began working at Tihar Jail in 1981 and was later promoted to the position of spokesperson and legal advisor of the jail. Since leaving Tihar Jail, he has worked with the High Court and Supreme Court as an advocate and member of the Delhi High Court Bar Association, accomplishing much to improve India's prison systems, from introducing Special Courts within the prisons to initiating video conferencing connections between jails and the court. He has also fought for gender equality within the prison system by ensuring that women are availed the same privileges of semi-open and open jail which are given to men. His efforts have earned him the India Vision Award for his achievements in the field of Prison Reforms and Administration. Gupta is the sole officer from the legal field to have received the President's Correctional Medal for Meritorious as well as Distinguished Services. This is his first book.

Sunetra Choudhury started her career at the *Indian Express* newspaper where she headed the city team. Three years later she moved to TV news and joined NDTV. After covering the 2009 election campaign travelling across the country on a bus for two months, she wrote *Braking News*. Her latest book *Behind Bars: Prison Tales of India's Most Famous* (2017, Roli Books) was the result of extensive interviews with high-profile inmates. In 2016, she received the Red Ink award and is the 2018 Jefferson Fellow. Most recently she is the recipient of Mary Morgan Hewett Award that recognizes the achievements of women journalists. Choudhury is currently the political editor at *Hindustan Times*.

In Praise of *Behind Bars: Prison Tales of India's Most Famous* by Sunetra Choudhury

'Based on extensive secondary research and detailed interviews with people who have spent time in jail as well as those who have worked in or on jails, Choudhury presents a series of stories which are nothing short of eye-opening – dare I say, even eye-popping – in their revelations.'

The Wire

'Choudhury has a fluid writing style and makes her book a compelling read. However, you may not want to breeze through it and instead take your time in savouring these 13 stories.'

Khaleej Times

'The author compels us to confront the agonies of people who are hauled up on charges of terrorism. But there are others too, who have been released and may be broken in body but not in spirit after several years inside. They come to life in these pages as evidence of injustice and failure of the system.'

Business Standard

'…*Behind Bars* is a fascinating effort, especially since the book is dripped in palpable anger against the many privileges of the elite, even inside jails. In that, it is a first draft of a sociological mapping of contemporary India, its many immoral famous ones, its heart-wrenching cruelties, the many individual sacrifices and the hidden secrets of its wealthy and powerful.'

The Hindu

'With unbelievable details of the life inside prison and the sorry state of hundreds of undertrials languishing in jails, this book questions the primary purpose of imprisonment – is it actually reform, punishment or just misusing the system we are a part of?'

Literary Yard

'These are heartbreaking stories – as is much of the book. Prison is heartbreaking. There is no soft landing in Tihar, no matter who you are. No matter how rich and famous you may be, jail is a terrible experience.'

Biblio

'This isn't a book for the faint-hearted with its stomach-churning descriptions of filth and violence but it casts a strong light on an area of darkness. It will prick your conscience and invite you to reflect on the conspiracy of silence that accompanies the gross human rights abuse in judicial custody.'

The Open Magazine

'With extraordinary details of the life inside prison and the sorry state of hundreds of undertrails languishing in jails, the book questions the primary purpose of imprisonment – is it actually reform, punishment or just misusing the system we are a part of.'

The Sunday Guardian

'In clean and engaging language, rich with detail and well-chosen adjectives, the book presents interesting facts about jail food, extraordinarily sincere jail employees as well as corrupt and perverted ones, rituals such as *mulakat* – and more.'

Hindustan Times

'Through Choudhury's smooth-flowing narrative, the book makes for an easy read. Her commendable access and references to chargesheets, court orders, research studies reassure the reader of her credibility, and builds faith in her content.'

Deccan Chronicle

BLACK WARRANT

CONFESSIONS OF A TIHAR JAILER

SUNIL GUPTA
SUNETRA CHOUDHURY

ROLI

First published by Roli Books in India, 2019
Eighth impression, 2025

Roli Books Pvt. Ltd
M-75, Greater Kailash II Market, New Delhi 110 048
Phone: +91 (011) 40682000
E-mail: info@rolibooks.com
Website: www.rolibooks.com

Also at Chennai & Mumbai

ISBN: 9788194206859

Typeset in ITC Galliard Std by Roli Books Pvt Ltd.

With the blessings of Almighty and my parents, this book is dedicated to my wife, Poonam, who pushed me to do more and better. And to my colleagues for restoring their faith in me.

CONTENTS

ACKNOWLEDGEMENTS

In the 35 years of my career in Tihar, I have learnt a lot from all my seniors from time to time, but there are a few who deserve special mention. The first IG Prisons, post Charles Sobhraj escape, P.V. Sinhari was the one who taught me to face any situation bravely, no matter how complicated the situation might get. Kiran Bedi, who was posted in Tihar in the year 1993, was a source of inspiration who would always surprise me with her out-of-the-box and thoughtful ideas. She followed the philosophy of Mahatma Gandhi, 'Hate the sin, not the sinner' and was a firm believer that a jail should be treated as a hospital for treatment of social deviants. She taught me to be intolerant towards any kind of injustice, no matter how influential the person imposing the injustice might be. Then came, R.S. Gupta who made me understand how important it was to work hard even if it meant working more hours. Ajay Agarwal, replaced R.S. Gupta, who was a mentor to me with whom I shared a very close bond. We didn't just discuss official matters but even our personal lives. He always motivated me to take prompt decisions, helped me overcome indecisiveness. My next boss, B.K. Gupta, taught me ways to deal with the corrupt and the sycophants. Then came Neeraj Kumar who made sure that I took everything with due seriousness and maintained officer like qualities. It was Sudhir Yadav who inculcated in me the need to take the reforms to the next generation.

I have also been really lucky to have my daughter, Himani and my son, Angad solidly beside me through the ups and downs of my career. Without their support and love, it wouldn't have been possible for me to fulfill the needs of my demanding job.

I will always be thankful to my friend Amit Khemka, senior lawyer, who helped me in my 2nd innings of life in establishing myself as a lawyer. It was he who pushed me to write my story. Credits are also due to Praveen Jain who took me to Priya Kapoor's office for narrating my experiences, and who after hearing my experiences, gave shape to this book.

This section would not be complete without thanking Sunetra Choudhury, who I had met 20 years back and was so impressed by her hard work and detailed reporting that I consider myself fortunate that she has co-authored this book.

Last but not the least, I would like to thank my wife Poonam, who has been the person most affected by my 24x7 work schedule and who supported me through all my ups and downs. Without her, I would have never completed the onerous responsibility of being the single law officer of 10 jails. I have, therefore, dedicated this book to her.

God Bless all!

Sunil Gupta

October 2019

~

THIS BOOK WOULD NOT HAVE BEEN POSSIBLE WITHOUT THE GUIDANCE of excellent lawyers like Ragini Ahuja and Rishabh Sancheti. I met Sancheti just once during a TV debate where I learnt about his interest in Surinder Koli, who was on death row for his role in the Nithari murders. When I started working on Sunil Gupta's story I realized that I needed to learn as much about death row inmates as I could. Sancheti put me in touch with Ragini Ahuja who I had never met before. And yet, out of the goodness of her heart and due to her conviction about the topic, Ragini listed out all the resources that I had to study. This included a list of judgements that I should read and also sending me the prison manuals of various states. The scanned pages of a pre-independence prison manual from Maharashtra was the most insightful piece of primary sourcing.

Senior lawyer Subodh Markandey was another generous resource for me. Markandey was sent to Tihar Jail in the late '70s by the Supreme Court to find out the truth about harassment and torture charges levelled by an inmate. When I called him out of the blue, he kindly looked through all his documents to find out his original report and had it sent over. It was again, an excellent source of information for this book, providing a context to the incidents that made up Sunil Gupta's story.

If you try to look up Maqbool Butt, the Kashmiri separatist who was hanged in Tihar, there is limited information. And so I am grateful to advocate R.M. Tufail, who was a young lawyer when he defended Butt. Tufail was able to help me piece together Butt's story and what happened in the days leading up to his hanging. Thanks also to Justice Mukul Mudgal and Dr. Anup Surendranath, who runs the Centre for Death Penalty.

Of course, the most important person to thank for this is Sunil Gupta, who decided to tell his story. In my mind, it is an act of courage that is seldom seen in public officials. I really hope that his words are read by his colleagues, all jail officials and judges and lawyers, so that they know the reality of our correction centres.

Priya Kapoor of Roli Books has always had a great ear for compelling stories and I thank her for choosing me to tell this one. Satbhan Singh played a crucial role in the research and transcribing interviews for the book and we thank him for his hard work and enthusiasm.

Many ask me how I am able to write books while also doing a very demanding day job. I think it's because I surround myself with a possé of supportive friends and family. So Ma and Papa, Ma and Baba, Sayantan, Vasudha and Viren, Neelanjana and Suranjan – I love and thank them all. Thanks also to my friends – Rasheed Kidwai who inspires with his prolific writing; Mansi, Mustafa, Nirmala, Naghma and Prachi and so many others who make me laugh and remind me of what's really important in life.

I told myself that after *Behind Bars*, I wasn't going to write another book so soon because it was too much hard work. I just wanted to vegetate and cuddle my kid when I wasn't chasing stories. But Sudeep Mukhia knows that nothing makes me happier than telling stories and so he pushed me to tell this one. The more amazing thing is that he's also inculcated this in our nine-year-old, Tiny, who kept asking when *Behind Bars 2* was going to come out. I hope when he's old enough to read it, he thinks it was worth seeing his mum glued to her screen for hours on end. Gauri, very efficiently, is his main care giver and we are both fortunate to have her in our lives. I'm just lucky to live with people who have enabled and inspired me to do more.

SUNETRA CHOUDHURY
October 2019

PROLOGUE

If someone told me I'd be writing a book with Sunil Gupta 20 years after I first met him, I'd find it as improbable as me doing time in Tihar jail. Sunilji, as we called him, was the archetypal government press relations officer. In 1999, when my colleague, photographer Praveen Jain, took me to meet him at the prison headquarters in Janakpuri, he provided a stark contrast to his surroundings. His office was stationed in an area with gunmen minding watch-towers, and a tall wall designed to discourage thoughts of the outside world, but Sunil Gupta easily laughed out loud during our conversation. He answered journalists' calls with a cheery greeting, and promised them an 'exclusive' story. If you went by Sunilji's version, then Tihar was actually a bit of downtime spa for those that had fallen out with society or even a reform boot camp for those who had strayed from the righteous path. Torture? No way. Custodial deaths? Impossible under his watch.

Sunilji understood that generations of reporters (and their readers) may not have read Dostoevsky but they were obsessed with *Crime and Punishment*. So, while he effectively deflected on stories of the horrors at Tihar jail, he would supply other fascinating details. The first story that I did for NDTV when I joined in 2003, was with Sunilji's help. The story was about an inmate who had cracked competitive exams while studying behind bars – an amazing story of human endeavour and from the prison authorities' perspective it showed them in a good light. For these stories, Sunilji would organize supervised trips inside Tihar. It was these visits that sparked off my obsession with prison tales.

In 2005 Sunilji gave me permission to visit Tihar to cover the plight of the children of women inmates. It was an incredibly moving story but while filming I remember being intensely conscious of the sanitized version of Tihar that we were exposed to – what was it really like? It's not like Tihar was filthy, but I remember the smell that permeated the place – it was a mix of stale, sweaty air and the stench of a toilet. Women hung around with vacant expressions and I was aware of the despair that surrounded me. Years later, post-2011, Sunil Gupta became even more sought after because journalists were keen to report about the white-collar executives and the politicians who had been imprisoned in the 2G spectrum allocation case. At that time, I was managing a team of reporters and would send them to Sunilji to find out what really happened when DMK leader M. Karunanidhi went to meet his daughter Kanimozhi in jail. He would give out slivers of information like how the former telecom minister A. Raja was spending his days studying his case files or what sport the real estate company Unitech owner Sanjay Chandra was playing with who. It kept reporters happy and it didn't do any damage to Tihar's reputation either.

Sunilji was so good at looking after Tihar's reputation that when Ram Singh, the ringleader of the rapists and murderers of Nirbhaya, was found dead under mysterious circumstances in 2013, there were very few news reports that questioned the role that Tihar officials played. By and large, the media accepted that the man who had led the brutality against the 23-year-old student had taken his own life. Compare this to when sexual offender Jeffrey Epstein committed suicide in a New York jail in July 2019, several investigating teams including the FBI questioned how a high-profile inmate could have taken his own life inside prison. In India, there was no such in-depth investigation. Maybe it was the effectiveness of the press relations officer or perhaps the public here is indifferent to what happens inside our prisons. This may explain why when the findings of the National Crime Records Bureau (2016) were released, there was no outrage that custodial deaths had doubled in just a year. From 115 deaths in 2015, there were 231 unnatural deaths in Indian prisons in the following year. That's a rise of 100.87 per cent, and yet, no one seems particularly perturbed.

These statistics, however, are national figures. As one prison official once said to me, every prison, in every district has a unique story of its own. Its superintendent is often a power centre unto himself, choosing which laws he abides by and which ones he simply ignores. In his 35-plus years at Tihar, Sunil Gupta had a ringside view of this and was an active participant in the workings of Asia's largest prison. Fortunately for me, his retirement in 2016 was a boon as it coincided with me writing my first book on jails, *Behind Bars: Prison Tales of India's Most Famous.* He gave me invaluable insights which I incorporated into the introduction of the book. 'We will also write my story, Sunetra,' he said to me when I went to meet him. I didn't think he ever would.

The reason why I was less hopeful about Sunil Gupta writing a book was that he just knew too much. He wasn't just the press relations officer for Tihar, but also the only legal officer of the prison, which means that he knew and played an active role in every decision that would have been taken through the years. Is it possible that he would come clean about it all? So I forgot about it until a year later when my publisher, Priya Kapoor, called. Our friend Praveen Jain had once again played facilitator and brought Sunilji to her so that she could help him bring out the story of Tihar told from his eyes. Priya thought I was the best person to write that story since I was already familiar with the dark world of incarceration.

I have to confess that I faced a major dilemma for several reasons.

The first was that I didn't want to be typecast with only being a prison diary writer. *Behind Bars* had been received well but I was emotionally strung out with my characters in the book. Was I ready to go down that path again so soon? Would I not be seen as trying to repeat it again by writing on the same theme?

The second, more important, reason was that I was not sure if I was the best person to tell Sunil Gupta's story. As a reporter, I had always written about the underdog. I could write about the terror accused and bring the story of his torture alive by getting into his shoes but should I really be telling the other side's story? It was true that Gupta had not been tainted by any scandal despite working in Tihar for so many years, but how could I be sure of the authenticity of his story? Personally, he was an amiable person but what was he actually like in his role as a prison officer?

So, I did my own investigation. I got in touch with Delhi Government informally as they are responsible for the administration of Tihar and asked if there were any red flags regarding Sunil Gupta. They confirmed that there were none. His former boss, an ex-director general of prisons wasn't too thrilled that I was writing his story (as opposed to his, I suppose) but again did not have any specific complaint against Sunilji. In addition, Praveen Jain who prompted Sunilji in telling his story is a journalist with high levels of integrity and swears by him.

All that remained now were my own doubts – I had written an entire book on the prison system so how different would his story be? But these concerns disappeared as soon as we met to hear Sunilji's story. In our very first meeting he told Priya and me about 'black warrants'. In my two decades as a journalist, this was the first time I had heard of such a thing. A black warrant is issued as soon as the inmate's mercy petition is rejected and is literally the message of death – indicating the time and date of when the hanging will be executed. Sunil Gupta had obtained eight such black warrants from the court – one for every hanging he had overseen. It gets its name from the black lines which frame the death warrant. Sunilji told us of the last few days of Afzal Guru, Maqbool Butt, Billa and Ranga and Indira Gandhi's assassins. For years, there has been a complete blackout of information about the hanging process. If you speak to lawyers like Ragini Ahuja and Rishabh Sancheti who have been fighting for those on death row, they will tell you how difficult it is to get any information. And here was Sunil Gupta, offering to tell us what actually happens when the state carries out a hanging. One reason why I think he is finally telling his story is because he is haunted by his experience. He shared poignant stories such as listening to the song '*Apne liye jiye to kya jiye*' from the 1966 movie, *Badal*, on loop because it reminded him of Afzal Guru's last hours. Sunilji sat with Afzal in his cell waiting for the designated time of hanging and during this time they sang this song together. This episode had clearly changed him forever. Afzal Guru's hanging was so sensitive, that the authorities did not even inform his family in Kashmir. Gupta provides us with a blow-by-blow account of the days before the hanging and the actual day itself. For the first time he discloses how the union minister at the time held one-on-one meetings with the Tihar director general to make sure that Afzal Guru was hanged without anyone getting a chance to raise an objection. It will become apparent to readers that Afzal's hanging was eerily similar to the 1984 hanging of another Kashmiri separatist leader, Maqbool Butt. Suniji's may be the only genuine account of what really happened in the two men's last days.

At the end, I was hooked because it was a very good story to tell. From 1981 to 2016, Sunil Gupta saw and interacted with key players in the country's criminal and legal history. Some of these events have never been written about before, some of them were only hearsay shrouded in secrecy and so through Gupta, we get a new perspective and an eye-witness who introduces us to some of the darkest characters, if not villains, of these three decades. One of the more endearing stories he shared with us was about how he loved playing badminton and would play with whichever inmate was interested. It sounds surreal but when he started playing, his partner was Charles Sobhraj and closer to retirement, it was Manu Sharma. For our readers, they may have been India's most notorious criminals, but for Gupta they were regular people. Sobhraj is the smooth-talking, good looking foreigner who plays a curious role in Gupta getting his job. Manu Sharma turns out to be the business brains behind Tihar's brand 'TJ's' becoming a commercial success.

Sunil Gupta reminded us of Billa and Ranga, crime partners who raped and murdered the siblings, Geeta and Sanjay Chopra in 1978. It was the case that changed the Capital forever, when people realized that Delhi was no longer safe. Sunilji was a rookie jailer when Billa and Ranga were hanged in 1982 and in this book he takes us through the countdown of a hanging. What he described of his first ever hanging got under my skin. To me the book is also about the pursuit of understanding what equips a human being with the skills of taking another's life? This question made me reach out to other jailers too – one from Dasna Jail in Uttar Pradesh and another key jailer from Maharashtra. The Maharashtra jailer was especially interesting because he had been a part of the last two hangings in the country – that of 26/11 terrorist Ajmal Kasab (in 2012) and the 1993 Mumbai blast conspirator, Yaqub Memon (in 2015). Unfortunately, he cannot be on record because he is still serving and is bound by official rules. However, he did share with me the difficulties they faced because Kasab and Menon's hangings were the first since 1995. 'There wasn't anyone in our staff who had done a hanging before this and so we all had to go through the books, our manual and then train everyone,' he said, adding, 'At each stage we faced a brand new set of problems and then figured out how to tackle them.' This jailer was a trained sociologist who joined the prison service as a natural extension of what he had learnt. However, Sunil Gupta was an old-fashioned jailer, who joined Tihar because it was a stable government job. Gupta's lot had to figure out how to handle correction and reform by trial and error – there was little training, manuals that remained more on paper and arbitrary standard operating procedures. For example, during one hanging, Gupta tells us that the convict's pulse refused to stop even after two hours. So what did they do? One guard apparently jumped into the hanging pit and pulled his legs until the convict's breath was finally forced out of him.

There are interesting insights into political events from Sunil Gupta's story. While we know about the thousands that were murdered and burnt alive in the anti-sikh riots of 1984 in Delhi, we know little about the actual men who assassinated Indira Gandhi. Gupta's account transports us to December 1984 when Delhi was yet to rouse itself from the murderous spree of attacks on the Sikh community. For me, just the revelation that all Sikh officers were removed from the Tihar workforce was enough to indicate just how much trust deficit there was at the time against the Sikh community. We also take great pride in the fact that even when a case is open-and-shut, such as 26/11 terror attacker Ajmal Kasab's, India stands for providing a full-fledged trial with the best legal minds providing defence. Was due process followed in Indira Gandhi's assassination case as well? The reading of the chapter is thought provoking. There are accounts of recent events too – what really happened to Nirbhaya's rapist and murderer Ram Singh? The narrative of suicide that has been the accepted truth till now is turned on its head by the events leading up to Ram Singh's death.

Behind Bars was the story of the wrongs that prisoners experience in the hands of the criminal justice system and the jailers; this book shows that jailers are also imprisoned and trapped by their own system. Underpaid and overworked, they are ill-trained and ill-equipped to handle the reform of prisoners. Most of their tortured selves become torturers themselves. The deal that Sunil Gupta and I had, was that he would have to tell me the truth, the complete story with all the warts exposed. You will, therefore, find that unlike other memoirs of government officers where the narrator stands above it all, as a saint and a hero, Sunil Gupta matter-of-factly admits when he got 'problematic' prisoners beaten up to ensure that he could continue to carry out his function. In the prison world, where convicts themselves are recruited to carry out administrative roles, you have to play jungle rules to survive, he conveys.

It is a compelling story but there is also a larger point that Sunilji and I are trying to make with this book. We hope that policy makers, the government and lawyers are prompted into action by what this account reveals. Take for instance Rajan Pillai's death. Twenty-five years and a judicial probe later, can the government honestly claim that there will not be another medical emergency death like Pillai's? A paper published in the SVP National Police Journal (December 2018) studied a model jail in Nahan, Himachal Pradesh and found that not only is there any CMO (Chief Medical Officer), a position that is mandatory to maintain in all jails, there is also no regular doctor in the prison. The article, written by an IPS officer, states that prisoners with serious conditions have to wait for visiting doctors and their condition often gets aggravated while waiting for the consult. Those fortunate to get a medical consult and recommendation for tests, have to rely on the availability of security guards to take them to the nearest hospital for a test. Inmates say that policemen are always in a hurry and if there is a queue, they bring them back without getting their tests done. This is the state of affairs in a model prison. In Haryana, things are worse. There are no lady doctors for women prisoners. Some jails like in Karnal, don't even provide sanitary napkins to women prisoners. They either have to buy their own, depending on whether their families can send them money, or get by with scraps of cloth, according to the Commonwealth Human Rights Initiative (CHRI).

We hope that the government wakes up to the immediate need for reinforcements in jails so that those that are working there are not so exhausted that they treat inmates with contempt. The

CHRI 2019 report on Haryana jails says in some areas there are staff vacancies of up to 44 per cent. No wonder, Sunil Gupta's stories are full of references of convicts or ***numberdars*** running jails. These ***numberdars*** maintain discipline and do the daily administration work according to Sunilji and, are invaluable to the functioning of jails. This less than ideal situation continues because oversight mechanisms like a monthly visit by the district and sessions judge does not take place in all the jails. (Source: Haryana Report, CHRI 2019.) In this regard, Sunil Gupta was an oddity. He genuinely wanted to help prisoners' reform and was happy with his job, something that neither his co-workers nor his family could understand.

It is the poor, the ones who don't have access to good lawyers and at times are not educated enough to know their rights, are left to the vagaries of the system. They are the ones who are exploited, tortured while the ones who are well off live in relative comfort. In the 1979 Supreme Court judgement on torture, also known as the Sunil Batra judgement, the judges quote Kuldip Nayar to describe how things stand for affluent inmates. Nayar was in Tihar from 1975 to 1977, as part of the crackdown on the media during the Emergency.

> Shri Kuldip Nayar, a responsible journalist with no apparent motive for mendacity nor inclination for subjectivity, in his book "In Jail". There was nothing in the author's view which money could not buy within the recesses of the prison campus. Giving a factual narrative, Shri Nayar wrote: one could get as much money as one wanted from outside – again at a price. There was a money order and mail service that perhaps was more dependable than what the postal department could offer. For instance, when a prisoner in my ward wanted two hundred rupees, he sent a note through a warder to his people in old Delhi and in less than twenty-four hours he had the money.

> He paid sixty-six rupees as collecting charges – thirty-three per cent was the prescribed "money order charge." ...Dharma Teja, the shipping magnate who served his sentence in Tihar, for instance, has thousands of rupees delivered to him, we were told. And if one could pay the jail functionaries one could have all the comforts one sought. Teja had all the comforts – he had an air cooler in his cell a radio-cum-record player set and even the facility of using the phone.... Haridas Mundhra, a businessman who was convicted of fraud, was another rich man who spent some time in Tihar. Not only did he have all the facilities, but he could also go out of the jail whenever he liked; at times he would be out for several days and travel even upto Calcutta. All this of course, cost a lot of money. An even richer prisoner was Ram Kishan Dalmia, he spent most of his jail term in hospital. He was known for his generosity to jail authorities, and one doctor received a car as a gift.
>
> But more than businessmen it was the smugglers jailed in Tihar who were lavish spenders. Their food came from Moti Mahal and their whisky from Connaught Place. They had not only wine but also women. "Babuji, not tarts but real society girls," one warder said. The women would be brought in when "the Sahiblog" went home for lunch, and their empty offices became "recreation rooms".

If you read the last two chapters of this book, you realize how little has changed even 40 years later. Perhaps the only thing that has changed is that instead of ordering food from Moti Mahal, rich inmates may have their own hotel which caters especially to jail officials and VIP inmates. I am uncertain if any jail official will ever challenge this status quo but am hopeful that having an insider's account will make it easier for High Court and Supreme Court judges to force all inmates to be treated equally.

A note to keep in mind for readers is that while I have tried to stay true to Sunil Gupta's voice in the book, it is fair to say that it is tempered by my own. As a journalist, it is challenging and daunting to become the voice of a career prison officer who has survived the system. I do hope I have succeeded.

Sunetra Choudhury
September 2019

Tihar Jail Complex, 1981

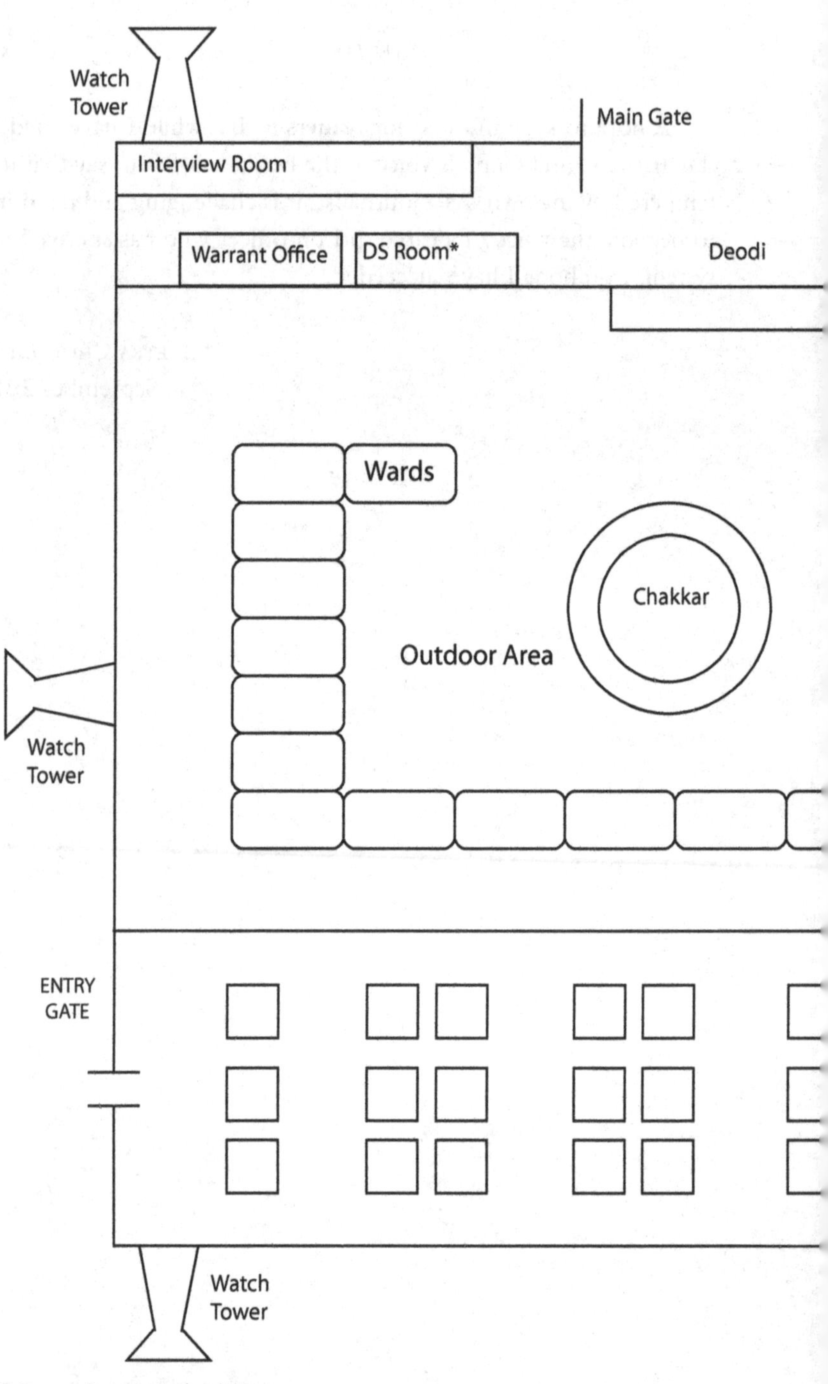

*SP Room: Superintendent's Room
*DS Room: Deputy Superintendent's Room
*Tel Exch: Telephone Exchange

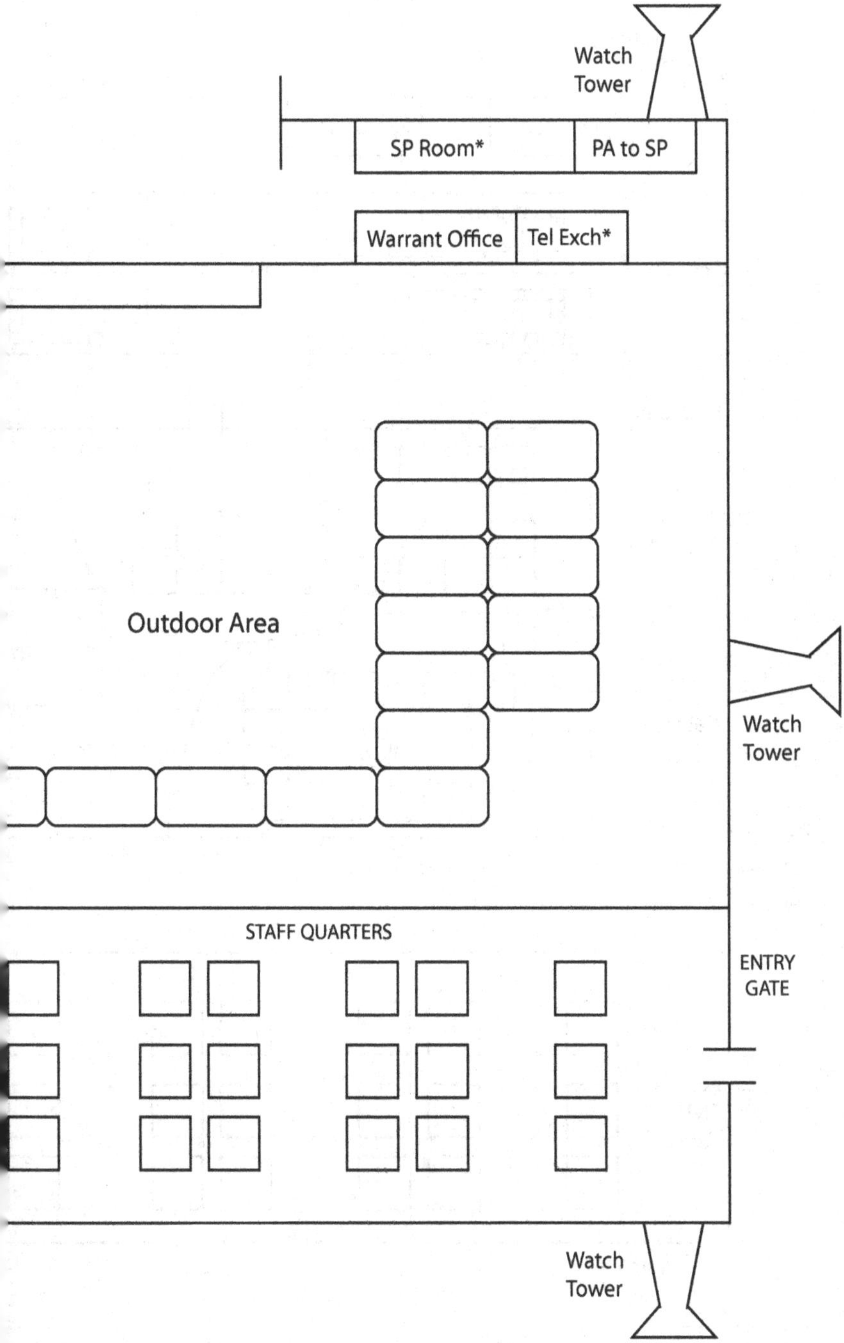

Watch Tower

SP Room*

PA to SP

Warrant Office

Tel Exch*

Outdoor Area

Watch Tower

STAFF QUARTERS

ENTRY GATE

Watch Tower

Tihar Jail Complex, 2019

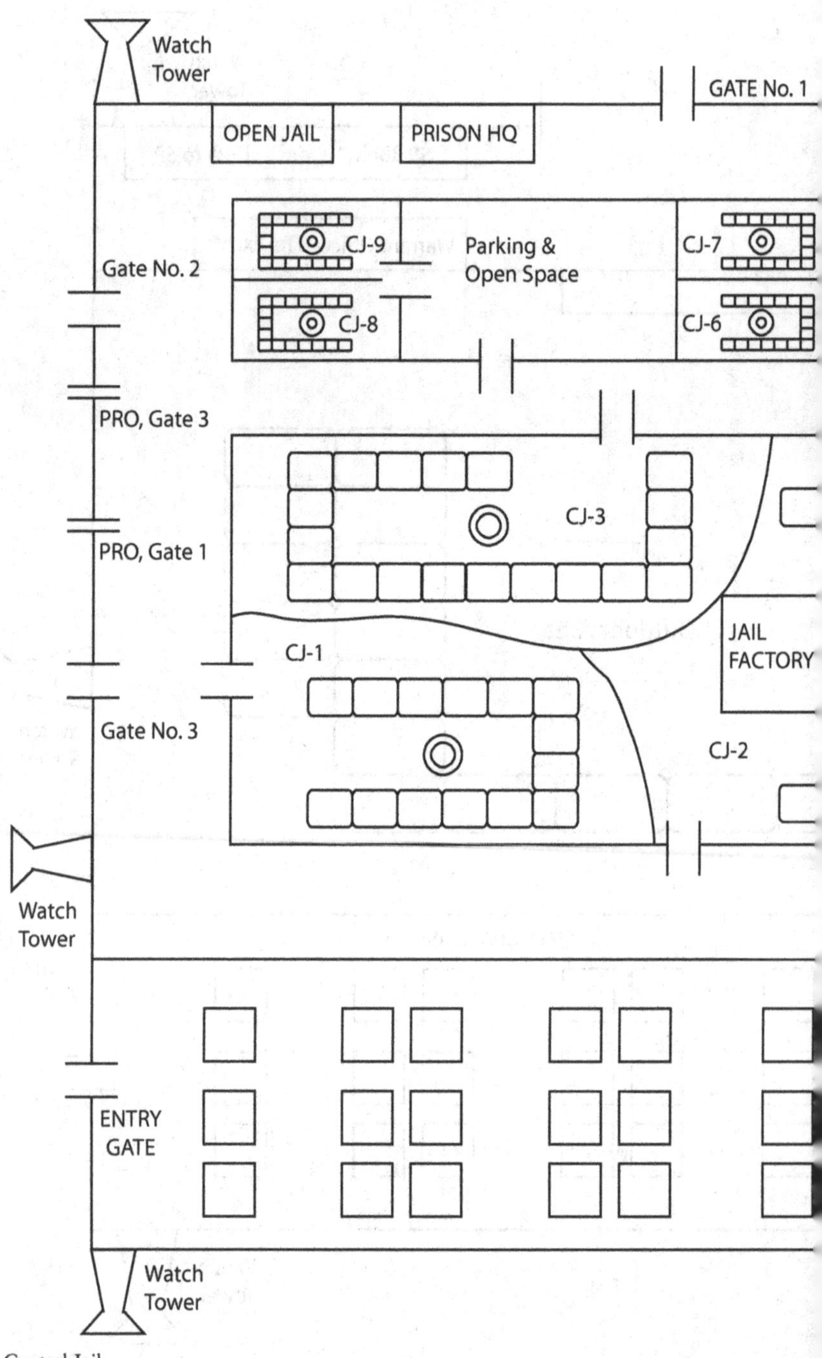

*CJ: Central Jail
*◎ Chakkar
*PRO Gate: For public entry
☐ Wards for inmates

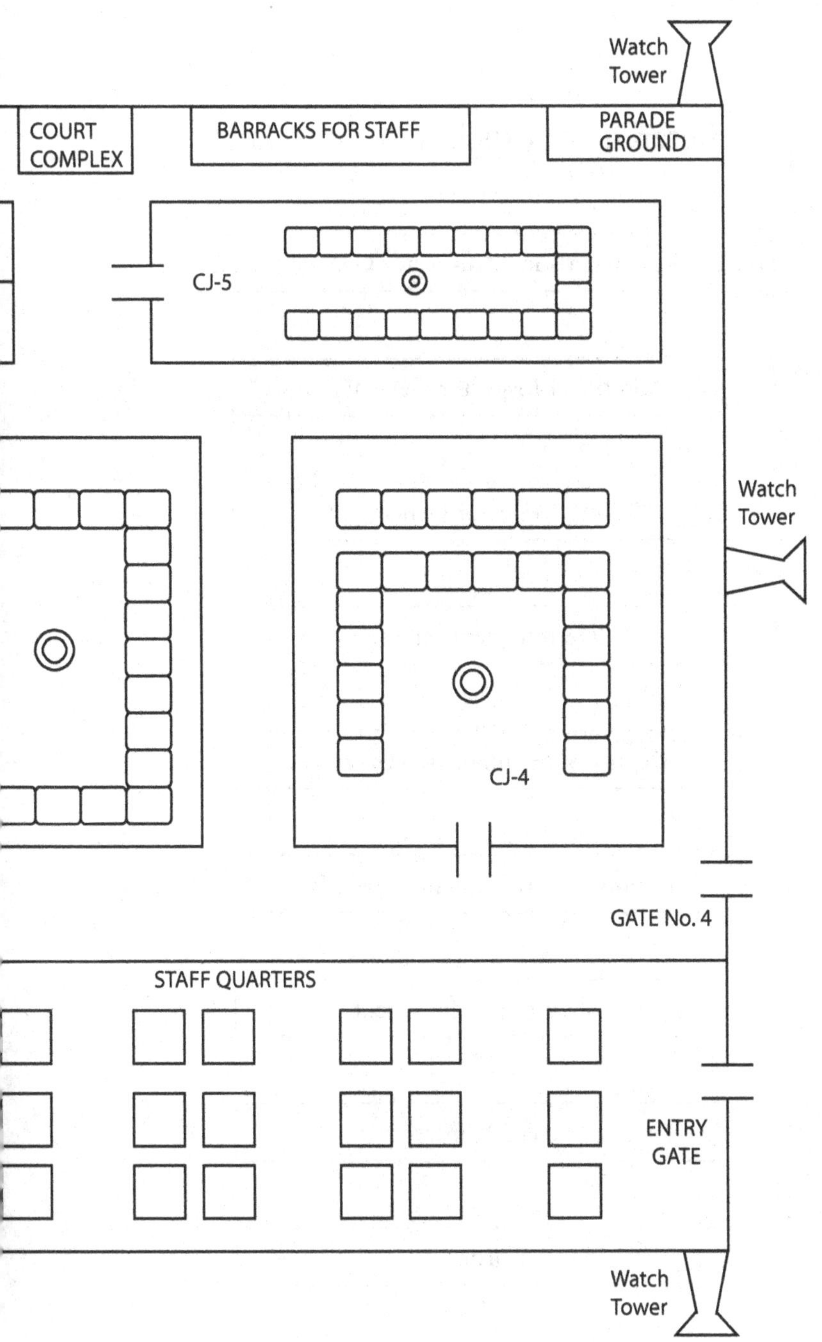
Watch Tower
COURT COMPLEX
BARRACKS FOR STAFF
PARADE GROUND
CJ-5
Watch Tower
CJ-4
GATE No. 4
STAFF QUARTERS
ENTRY GATE
Watch Tower

Hierarchy of officials in Tihar Jail

Director General (Prisons)/Inspector General (Prisons)

Additional Inspector General (1)

Deputy Inspector General (2)

Superintendent Jail (18)

Deputy Superintendent (Grade I)

Deputy Superintendent (Grade II)

Assistant Superintendent

Head Warder

Warder

DAY 1: HOW CHARLES SOBHRAJ SECURED MY JOB

May 8, 1981 The very first day that I reported for duty I got an inkling about the neurosis of my new co-workers. I began to realize that dealing with incarceration and the incarcerated does strange things to the mind.

I remember the date clearly because my life changed in ways I could not have imagined. Clutching my offer letter, I arrived at the office of B.L. Vij, the then superintendent of jails in Tihar. I had already resigned from the Northern Railways which had been okay as far as jobs go, but it came with a major cause of concern for me. Being a railways man meant that I would have to live my life on the road, or the tracks. The unpredictability of a transfer at any and all times did not really appeal to me. So when I saw a job opening in Tihar, I thought it was the perfect opportunity to begin a life in the national capital. I was 24 years old.

Of course, no one in my family shared my sentiments. We were three brothers and two sisters and I was the fourth one with a sister younger than me. Among the five siblings, there was a nuclear scientist from IIT and a college professor. The thought of their Hindu College-educated son going to work among *chors* (thieves) *uchakkes* (ruffians) was not at all appealing to my parents. What made things worse was that the newspapers at the time were full of stories about Tihar Jail that terrified them: 'Inmate threatens jail staffer' or worse still, 'Inmate kills Jailer'.

'Is this why you studied BSc and Law?' I was asked.

I certainly did not study science and law to join the family business. I mean who wanted to spend their life dealing with FMCG products in Ludhiana? I wanted a challenge and Asia's largest prison promised this in abundance. The railways relieved me of my services on 7 May and the very next day, I turned up at the West Delhi jail.

I was keen to start as the assistant superintendent of prison (ASP) and quite proud that I had sailed through the interview board and landed this job that seemed ideal. I went straight to the superintendent's room and announced my intention to join, hoping that he would direct me to someone who would help me complete all the formalities. B.L. Vij took one look at me and simply said, 'There's no vacancy for the post of an ASP here.'

I was astounded, not quite sure if I had heard him right. Did he look at my thin-bordering-on-underweight physique and dismiss me as not being tough enough for the job? Did he not like my face? What was going on here?

I tried to calm the panic that was taking over me. 'But sir, I have my appointment letter. How can there be no vacancy?' I said, hoping he would not be further angered by the dangerously high pitch of my voice.

'You should have asked before leaving the railway job,' he answered, shortly. He was clearly impatient with me challenging his authority. I sat sweating more from panic than the May heat. I went over the entire process in my head, trying to work out where I had gone wrong. I received the offer a month ago but did not join immediately because I needed to serve the notice period. Was this going to cost me this job? How could I be left bereft of both jobs?

Suddenly, I thought of something.

'Sir, did you get a call from someone?'

'No, I didn't.'

'Didn't R.P. Singhal, IAS call you?'

As soon as I said this, I noticed an instant change in his manner. He asked me to wait outside his office.

I didn't know R.P. Singhal, but I remembered his name from our CBSE school text books because it was printed in the preface as he was the chairman of the education board. I figured that if his name was important enough to be imprinted in every schoolboy's memory it would impress Vij too. He also happened to be from the same *gotra* (caste) as me so I figured, if he ever cross-checked my reference, maybe I could persuade this mythical R.P. Singhal.

Anyway, while waiting outside for my fate to be decided, I spotted a smartly dressed man wearing a tie and jacket. He could have been in his mid-20s and looked quite incongruous to Tihar Jail's atmosphere. Somehow he also looked familiar.

'Yes, what brings you here?' he asked me in English. I explained the strange situation I had found myself in.

'Don't worry. I can help you,' he said and with this quiet assurance he went inside B.L. Vij's office.

An hour or so later, the well-dressed man came out of the room with a letter which stated that I had been inducted as an ASP. Handing me this letter, he walked away.

I was elated but wanted to know who this powerful man was, so, I stopped a passerby. 'He's Charles Sobhraj. He is the "super IG" of the jail, he runs everything here.' The man who was serving out a long jail sentence for committing multiple murders and was wanted in a number of countries across the world, had played a crucial role in getting me the job I held for the rest of my working life. After that I saw many others getting harassed when they came for jobs. Maybe, it was their bad luck that they did not bump into Sobhraj. It was later that I got to know that you could not be just a regular guy without any connections and hope to get a job at Tihar. There were 10 people who joined at the same time as me – and all had powerful connections – including one who was recommended by the Lok

Sabha Speaker and another by no less than the home minister. Also I found that B.L. Vij was known to be biased towards people from his home state of Haryana.

But all this came much later. At that time, I was just happy to have finally managed to join the ranks of Tihar and was keen to begin work.

~

The Tihar Jail complex is spread across 200 acres. In those days there were just two parts to it – the Central Jail and the Camp Jail. The Camp Jail, which is now Jail number 4 of Tihar, was where those who were agitating were sent. The Central Jail was our main place of work and I remember the impressive, forbidding iron gates at the entrance which was always manned by an armed guard. The staff quarters were outside this area. In 1981, half of this area had been taken over for jail buildings while the rest was open fields and staff quarters. The quarters were separated from the jail by a wall which blocked any kind of view. I remember when I came in to work for the first time a rifled guard saluted me. This thrilled me immensely and I boasted about it to my family that evening.

When you go past this entry, you arrive at a kind of reception area of the jail. Up till here your freedom is still yours. On the left is the superintendent's office and that of his secretary. On the same side is the very important warrant office that tracks the dates a convicted prisoner gets bail or is released. Opposite this, to the right side of the entrance, are the offices of other jail officials and the warrant office for undertrials. From there, a corridor leads to the interview room, where families are allowed to meet prisoners. We would call it the *mulaqat jangla*, *jangla* being a reference to the mesh that separated the prisoner and their families or lawyers. Between the left and right areas, and just facing the entrance is the *deodi* area of the jail. This was where you had to check in and out of jail. Cross this gate and go past the sentry here and you were now in jail.

Past this gate is the *chakkar,* the nerve centre for the entire prison operation. This is an open space with a couple of rooms where the jail officials have their office. Around it are the wards for inmates and a large kitchen catering to them. Cell-kitchen-*chakkar*, this was the world as inmates knew it. When I first went there, the chief head warder or the in charge of the *chakkar* warmly invited me in and gave me *jaljeera* to drink. I was not expecting such a welcome because in my mind at that time, frills such as these were an anomaly in jail. Of course, I did not know then that money could buy you anything in jail.

Sitting there, sipping *jaljeera*, I witnessed the strangest things unfolding around me. While my host was plying me with pleasant refreshments, right in front of us, prisoners were being beaten. I learnt quickly that no rules applied in the *chakkar*. It was one place where there were no CCTV cameras and would therefore serve as the place to beat those who were seen to be errant or needed to be taught a lesson. While I could not help but stare at the beatings, no one else seemed perturbed. Men who appeared to be potentially dangerous inmates were wandering everywhere and frankly, I was scared. It was as if no one was in control and if the system was working, it was all *Ram bharose*. These dangerous inmates, instead of being locked up, also seemed to play the role of being 'bouncers' for jailers. The jailers sat cowering in their rooms, and these prisoners stood guard outside. I learnt later that this wasn't just an ornamental tactic. There was a real fear of officials being beaten up by inmates if they got really unruly, so guarding them was necessary.

At another end of the *chakkar*, a few prisoners were on a hunger strike. When I asked what the reason for this was, I was told that a prisoner who had been serving a life sentence, Madan Lal, had died after being beaten in custody. Those on strike were demanding that the matter be probed and action be taken against his killers. Again, my naivety was exposed. I didn't understand why they needed to strike to demand an inquiry – surely it should have been the norm. I would soon learn that while it was the norm, the sub-divisional magistrates who conducted these inquiries would always favour the jailers in their reports and the truth would not be recorded. I kept the questions to myself and stared with amazement at my new world.

Looking back, I should not have been so surprised at the disorder that I saw on that first day. There were no specially trained professionals working in jails at the time. Officers from Sales and Tax, Land and Building and even *patwaris* (junior land officials) served as the prison staff. There was no training, you learnt on the job. My own training was not done by any staff members but by two inmates Charanjit and Dhumi, who were both convicted of murder and serving life terms. Charanjit was in prison for murdering his girlfriend and Dhumi for killing a relative. They both served as orderlies for the superintendent and the deputy superintendent. I quickly learnt that they were both experts at jail rules. They taught me how to check a warrant from the court, which particulars were to be entered in the records and how to scan court notices extremely carefully. They also taught me what would become my primary job at the *qaidi* (convict) seat – how to free a prisoner once he is allowed to walk free. They took me through the formalities and legalities to be completed before an inmate is freed. I wasn't the only one; my entire batch was trained by them.

We later realized their ulterior motives for being such efficient trainers for all of us – they had devised a system where they would tip off certain prisoners about their court dates. This is how it worked. Suppose a warrant was issued for a particular inmate to travel to UP. If that inmate patronized Charanjit or Dhumi, they would make that warrant disappear. I know it sounds strange – why would anyone want their warrant to disappear? If you were a history-sheeter or a person who was criminally-inclined and wanted in various parts of the country, you were bound to have endless warrants from several courts. This meant that even if you served out your sentence, or got bail in one case in one part of the country like in Tihar, you would not be freed, but sent to the next court to face the second trial and the entire rigmarole would begin again. So, for instance, an accused

Maoist like Kobad Ghandy was in Tihar from 2009 to 2016 when he was acquitted of conspiracy of terror charges. But there were 20 other cases pending against him so instead of walking out of jail he went to the next city which was Hyderabad to face trial for the charge in that state. Ghandy was a high-profile convict so it was not going to be possible for anyone in the jail, however big the bribe, to hide his pending cases. But for small time criminals, Charanjit and Dhumi worked their 'magic'. For a small fee, they would make warrants from another court or city, disappear. So, thanks to them, a burglar wanted in Delhi and Faridabad, would be able to get away and walk free if his production warrant from the Faridabad court went missing. It was all a part of the jail machinery but we were oblivious to it until we became entrenched jail hands ourselves.

The Delhi Prisons Act of 2000 states that all jails have to have a training institute, but till today Tihar does not have one. When inmates train officers it is obvious where the power centre really lies. Officers with no special training did not know about jails and rules, and neither did they make any effort to educate themselves. They were happy functioning as *babus* where they would sit in an office and work on files and never even visit the actual prison compound. Inevitably, jails were run by long-term convicts or *numberdars* who were chosen on the basis of good behaviour. Formalized in the prison rules and jail manuals, they had the same status of a public servant and would carry out most duties like doing a headcount of inmates in the morning and evening. The evening count would end with lock-in which happened quite late those days, at 11 or 11.30 pm. Today lock-in happens much earlier, around 8 pm for men and even earlier for women inmates. There is no official early deadline for women but apparently women do get locked up earlier. In Delhi jails, dinner is served at 5 pm, which means lock-in is even earlier. Every cell would be sealed for access at night other than the *mulaiza* ward, which is where new inmates are kept when they enter the jail. When they first arrive, they are given a medical test and kept away from the hardened criminals that may be in jail. Rules forbid officials from approaching any cell after lock-in unless an inmate is seriously ill or there is a fire.

'Lock-out' happened at 6 am, soon after the inmates were woken up. If the counting tallied with the number from the evening before, all was good – no one had escaped or died overnight. In those days when I joined the situation was so bad that whenever lock-in and lock-out was successful, officials used to thank their stars. There was so much lawlessness at that time: violent fights would break out, someone would run away, anything could happen. That was the reason why lock-out would be punctual but lock-ins would inevitably be delayed. It was quite normal to be spending time looking for an inmate. So when everyone was found where they were supposed to be, we would note in our daily report quite literally – *sab acha* (all is well).

The release orders, announcing the bail or acquittals of prisoners would come from court in the evening between 5-6 pm and from high courts, later around 9-10 pm. A jail with a population of around 2,000 and a floating population of those who were brought in for petty crimes would also have a daily inflow of those that were released or brought in by court orders. So the evening was primetime for *numberdars* and other jail staff acting as agents for officers. Every evening, they would collect money from family members who had come to receive the released prisoners. Those who could pay would be released immediately but others who could not, were detained. This was the unwritten norm and a steady source of income for all.

Even if a prisoner was not being released, he could still be harassed by the *numberdar*, who would go around extorting money. The terror unleashed by them stemmed from the fact that they were not answerable to anyone. As they were already serving out jail sentences, the maximum one could do was to end their *numberdaari* in jail and make them ordinary prisoners. Most of the beatings that would take place in jail would be done by them. And if someone felt wronged, there were not too many people to take your grievances to. There were no senior jail officers around at night to register a complaint of an excess committed by a *numberdar*. The ones who were around were hand-in-glove with them or simply did not care. Inevitably every evening, the alarm would go off because older and more entrenched prisoners had attacked other inmates. The alarm, signalling an emergency, would tell all staffers to rush to tackle the situation. Often it was misused because an alarm also gives jail officials the right to use force in the pretext of bringing the situation under control. In 1988, Delhi administration rewrote the jail rules and stripped *numberdars* of their public servant status. There was a massive backlash to this revision in the rules because *numberdars* claimed they had earned this right by their good behaviour and scrapping the system was anti-reformist.

Of course, the violence wasn't just inflicted by *numberdars*. Drug abuse in the form of Mandrax (a sedative), was prevalent and at times the users had blade wars, or when they were high, they would hide and not be found for hours. If you have watched the hit movie *Sholay*, you will know what I'm talking about. Copying a scene from the film when the inebriated hero Dharmendra climbs on top of a water tank demanding that the heroine Hema Malini agree to marry him or else he would jump, some inmates would also climb a tree or hide in a water tank after getting high on Mandrax. Once, an inmate demanded that a judge be called to hear him before he got out. All in all, Tihar was a mess. The *Indian Express* would report on the dismal state of affairs every single day. We called the *Indian Express* 'Tihar Express' because we featured so prominently in their coverage.

~

During my orientation, I got to know Charles Gurmukh Sobhraj a lot better. He was never locked up in a cell and could mostly be found sitting in the administrative office. My colleagues regaled me with stories of how very influential he was, not knowing that I had also been a beneficiary. To say that Sobhraj was enjoying life in Tihar was an understatement. Unlike other inmates, there was no lock-in or lock-out for him. He could go wherever he wanted to and he interacted and treated the superintendent and his deputy as his peer. No one stopped him from doing anything. In fact, the ***Indian Express*** carried a story in September 1981 which said Tihar Jail is ruled by Charles Sobhraj. The People's Union of Civil Liberties (PUCL) report that came out that year gave further details:

> Inside the jail, Sobhraj and his friends set up their own dens from where they ran their business – dealing in narcotics and selling drugs and liquor. Sobhraj and his friends would beat up anybody who would dare to put up resistance. The condition of the jail deteriorated to the extent that docile prisoners became target of abuse by the hardened criminals. Vij and his cronies who had managed to keep higher officers in the administration in good humour, looked the other way when criminals went on the rampage inside.

Sobhraj's friends that the report referred to were Sunil Batra, Vipin Jaggi and Ravi Kapoor – all three jailed for the conspiracy to rob a bank. They were well-off, educated and scamsters. They would freely roam the jail grounds looking for an opportunity to take someone for a ride. They exploited their influence with the authorities to make a quick buck wherever they could. If someone did not have a lawyer, they would extract money from him to write out a court application. They would file human rights cases against those officials who did not fall in line or were not in favour with them. It was for this reason that you find their names all over the Supreme Court judgements on jail reform in the 1980s. Some of the judgements referred to their attempt to improve prison conditions, while others dealt with their misadventures.

In the Rakesh Kaushik judgement delivered by the Delhi High Court, the judges do not refer to Charles Sobhraj by name but said this about the 'foreign convict who was wanted by Interpol':

> This foreigner is especially encouraged and protected by the Superintendent and Deputy Superintendent. He can be seen visiting these officers and holding private conferences in the private retiring rooms at the back of their offices almost daily. So much so, that the Deputy Superintendent even allows this foreign convict to consummate sexual intercourse in his private back room from time to time – the Deputy Superintendent performing as though he were this foreign-convict's pimp. Naturally, for conceding such and many more extra facilities, both the Superintendent and Deputy Superintendent charge heavy amounts from his foreign convict, who has now struck rich after the publication of his two books.

Sobhraj's girlfriend at the time was reported to be Shireen Walker who he summoned to India. She stayed at a five-star hotel while she was in Delhi. The PUCL mentioned in their report that Shireen Walker met him for hours in the official's room over six days.

Sobhraj began visiting my office. But first let me first tell you how I came to occupy the specific office of a legal officer. My bosses realized I had a law degree and since there was so much bad press which in turn led to questions from the judiciary, I was given the responsibility of responding to the legal notices. I was happy because it meant I would be away from the oppressive conditions of the jail and instead attending court hearings. As I had no staff for typing, jail officials turned to their usual pool of human resources. They assigned Captain R.S. Rathaur to work with me. According to the former army officer, he had been falsely accused of spying for Pakistan in what was called the Samba Spying case. The army court-martialled him and he spent 16 years in Tihar. He used his time in jail to write a book titled, *The Price of Loyalty,* and also proved to be an excellent typist for me. Tihar doesn't hire typing staff specifically and if they do, their work is extremely unsatisfactory. But inmates would work until 10 or 11 pm and the quality of their work was very good.

Whenever Rathaur drafted letters on my behalf, they would be in such good English that even my superintendent could not understand certain words. He assumed I had superior language skills due to my law education and would quickly sign the letters. Actually, it was all the work of Captain Rathaur and later, Charles Sobhraj. There were many reasons why such work was so attractive for inmates. First, they would escape the tyranny of bad jail food. We would order special food for them which made a world of difference. Second, their family could visit them properly. There was none of the usual jostling and waiting around, the bribery of petty officials and *numberdars*. Captain Rathaur's family could meet him comfortably at his workplace, which was my room. The biggest advantage, however, was the one I identified with. Going from an army captain to a typist may be a comedown in life, but it was still better than being locked up in a cell. In my office, he could access newspapers, had access to the library and perhaps for a few minutes, he felt like a free man. Not surprisingly, the position of a typist was highly sought after amongst the qualified inmates.

But I have digressed. My office had many law books and Sobhraj would drop in and hang around to read them. Initially, I was sceptical and tried to shoo him away. 'Don't come to the office so frequently,' I said, adding that he must bring the slip that was required for any inmate's movement outside his cell. I was also concerned that he was taking advantage of having helped me with my appointment letter with Vij and would want his pound of flesh. But he was so used to moving in and out of various offices, I don't think he ever took my objections seriously. He continued to come to my office, always without the mandatory slip. Often he would boast that if I ever needed to get some work done by the superintendent, I shouldn't hesitate to tell him. The thought of being further obliged to him was terrifying. However, I got tired of telling him off and soon he became a regular at my office along with Captain Rathaur.

His method of influencing staffers was quite subtle unlike some of the other inmates. I remember one early attempt by another inmate when I was relatively new. He approached me and said, 'Sir you have two sisters? One is studying and the other one is a teacher?' I nodded and asked how he knew. Without answering, he said, 'I also know that you are one of three brothers, out of which one is a scientist and one is an administrative officer.' When the prisoner told me specific details about my family, I got worried. He wanted a change in his sleeping arrangement and I understood that indirectly, he was threatening me – 'Get it done otherwise I know where your loved ones are!'

But Sobhraj didn't resort to such petty or crude threats. He had already ensured that his sleeping environs were the least grim of all inmates. His cell measured 12 by 10 feet and he did not have to share it with anybody. If he worked in our offices, he also had the luxury of 'servants' in jail – C class prisoners who would massage him, wash his clothes and even cook for him. I am not sure about Sobhraj but other high-profile prisoners would also use their 'servants' to service them sexually. Jail officials were aware of this, but since it was deemed consensual, they turned a blind eye.

In his cell, Sobhraj had a shelf full of books and had arranged the furniture he was allowed – a chair, table and a bed – so well, it looked more like a studio apartment. And unlike all other inmates, he had the freedom to cook his own food. He could do all this because he paid jail staffers or he did jobs for them that no one else could. For instance, he would draft petitions for both prisoners and jailers. The petitions drafted by him, often turned out to be effective, even more than the ones drafted by actual lawyers. It's not that he took decisions for us but if we had to make a case, say to convince the court that we were doing our work effectively, Sobhraj knew how to build a case and draft our responses. These were not very complicated legal matters. Things like, if any staffer received a summon from the court and had to respond to it, Sobhraj would formulate the perfect response and of course if they needed money, he would give them that too. No wonder, Sobhraj considered himself a leader of both the prison staff and inmates.

It was not very long before word got around of his rising prominence in Tihar. Soon after the *Indian Express* had branded him the 'King of Tihar', the jail had an unexpected visitor. Barely four months after I joined, I was on duty one September evening in 1981 when a guard came running to me at around 7.30 pm. He said, 'Sir, the home minister has arrived. Should I allow him in?' It sounds ridiculous but it was drilled into every guard to not let anyone into Tihar without permission from the jail authorities regardless of who that visitor may be. Even so, I could not believe that he had kept Home Minister Giani Zail Singh waiting! 'Let him in, let him in. You are going to get us both sacked!' I said and rushed to receive him at the gate where the minister told me he wanted to inspect the jail.

To say it was an unusual request was an understatement. But Gianiji meant business. He directed me to take him to the cell in which Charles Sobhraj was kept. I did as I was told but was very anxious that I should not be the one doing this job. My boss, the deputy superintendent (DSI) of the jail should have been there instead. But his regular routine was to stroll in around 8.30 pm, so that he could collect a 'fee' from all those who were being freed that day. As soon as that job was done and all those who were freed, had left by 10.30 pm, he would leave too.

This routine worked well but today the minister had other plans. Meeting Sobhraj, he asked him in Hindi, '*Tum kaise ho? Tumhein yahan koi taqleef to nahin hai?*' I translated for Sobhraj, 'He is asking about your well-being.' Sobhraj gave a straightforward response in English that he was alright and that he didn't have any complaints. He also told the minister that he read books all day and drafted petitions for other prisoners as a form of killing time. After chatting for a couple of minutes or more, Gianiji wanted to visit a ward. I took him to an adjoining one. There, suddenly two prisoners, Bhajji and Dina, started shouting, '*Chacha Nehru Zindabad. Yeh Chacha Nehru ki jail hai. Yahan sub kuch milta hai.*' (Long live, Nehru! This is Nehru's jail. We get everything here.) I was a little relieved because they were not exactly saying anything negative. In fact, Gianiji seemed happy that he had encountered two patriots! His secretary took the two prisoners aside to a corner – I could not hear their exchange but was later told that the prisoners explained to the secretary exactly what they meant by 'We get everything here' – drugs, alcohol, and anything they could ever want. Apparently they also revealed, 'If you want to get somebody killed, that's also very easy and attainable.' After the conversation with the secretary, the prisoners were taken away and the minister's visit to Tihar was wrapped up in half an hour.

During this half hour, I had been desperately trying to reach my boss, Deputy Superintendent O.P. Sharma to tell him to get here quickly. The deputy superintendent did return but his attitude was one of nonchalance. He did his work, freed the prisoners and left. His boss, B.L. Vij, whose bungalow was next door, chose to work mostly from home leaving it all to Sharma – but this worked against him that day. The next day, as expected, Giani Zail Singh's visit featured prominently in the newspapers. The report said the prisoners gave the minister's secretary an empty alcohol bottle as a demonstration of how easy it was to access contraband. We were used to adverse news reports, but this was very serious. Two days after this incident, the Ministry of Home Affairs suspended six people – I was one of them. Along with me, were three other officers, Deputy Superintendent O.P. Sharma, Deputy Superintendent S.N. Trikha and Assistant Superintendent S.K. Kukreja.

I was shocked. The reason on paper was 'relaxed supervision' but I was not going to accept that charge. They questioned me how two sloganeering inmates made their way into an area when it was out of bounds for them. I told them I was escorting the minister so how could I be held responsible for other lapses like the inmates' movement. After I fought back, I was recalled to duty in one-and-a-half months. Others were repatriated to their own cadres and were subjected to suspension and departmental action. Their suspension, including that of my boss, O.P. Sharma, continued for many years. I wondered why I was embroiled in their mess and I was convinced it was because I was not liked by O.P. Sharma or B.L. Vij. Basically, I was not part of the Haryana coterie. Being part of the coterie meant you would not be made to run around, you would be given all the plum positions and life would be easier. This incident featured prominently in the PUCL report of that year:

> Then came the famous visit by the Home Minister, Mr Zail Singh, to the jail. He was offered a bottle of liquor by a drunken prisoner. Apart from this, he saw many other goings-on in the jail. He was shocked and enraged. But even the Home Minister did not order immediate penal action against Vij and his company. Five days later, the *Indian Express* again came out with a report about the Home Minister's visit to the jail which was kept secret: There was no other way. Mr Zail Singh had to order the suspension of two jail officials S.N. Trikha and O.P. Sharma. Vij, who had links in the Prime Minister's secretariat, activated his contacts and managed to get out of the difficult situation. Despite this scandalous episode, Vij remained in his place.

During my suspension, Sobhraj kept in touch with me. He offered money if I needed it. I told him, '*Bhaiya*, I don't need any money,' and told him off for even suggesting it. But I regretted it because he was simply reaching out to show me sympathy. And was it really his fault when he had freely given money to almost the entire jail staff and they never said no? I am proud to say that in his book, Sobhraj has written that there was only one officer that he could not buy for money. This was the kind of challenge I signed myself up for when I came to Tihar.

BREAKOUT OF THE 'BIKINI KILLER'

The stories of Charles Sobhraj's fiefdom inside Tihar may be legendary but they are nothing compared to the story of his escape from prison. All these years, I have maintained my silence about the multiple accounts of how the 'Bikini Killer' (so called because his victims' bodies were apparently found dressed in bikinis in Thailand) managed to dupe us all. But it is now time to set the record straight.

Sobhraj's jailbreak happened almost exactly a decade after he came to Tihar on 6 July 1976, which was years before I joined the jail administration. Even though he was wanted for a string of murders in multiple countries including India, he was also held for extradition proceedings and that too for trying to drug a group of 60 French tourists. That story, too, is incredible. The man who had fooled people all over the world finally got caught when his attempt to drug and rob 60 tourists at Delhi's Vikram Hotel went awry. The dosage that he administered to them was a little off and his victims got diarrhoea. Suspecting Sobhraj, they made the hotel call the police to question and arrest him. So in this case, Sobhraj's plan literally went down the toilet.

Of course, this was not the only case he was serving time for. He was charged with the 3 January 1976 murder of an Israeli tourist called Alan Aren Jacobs in Varanasi. He had used sedatives in this case as well. Sobhraj and another foreigner, a woman, checked into Hotel Natraj in Varanasi, along with Jacobs and an Indian man called Mohan Lal. While Mohan Lal and Jacobs shared a room, Sobhraj and the woman pretended to be a French couple called Mr. Nipier Ponant and Mrs. Nicole Ponant. The next day, the two checked out of the hotel saying that they preferred staying at the Clarks hotel instead. They did this but checked in pretending to be Mr. and Mrs. Alan Jacobs this time and used Jacobs's forex traveller's cheques to make the payment. On 5 January, they returned to Hotel Natraj and asked for Jacobs and Mohan Lal. The hotel staff said that the last time Jacobs was seen alive was when a hotel employee, delivering water to his room, saw Sobhraj handing him a pill. Hours later, the couple and Mohan Lal were gone and Jacobs was found poisoned with zinc phosphate.

Despite this series of drug-and-dupe (and sometimes even murder) cases, Sobhraj's strong legal representation meant he was almost about to be freed and handed over to Thailand, when he made a run for it. The press's theory was that he only ran away because he wanted to escape facing trial and punishment for the string of murders in Thailand, but that is not what he told me.

16 March 1986 was a Sunday and my day off. Later when I heard the story so many times I felt as if I had actually been there. The first person to raise an alarm was Constable Anand Prakash arriving at the jail quarters with his face covered in a thick cloth. The reason he had his face covered was revealed only later. When he rang the doorbell at the deputy superintendent of prison's office, he could hardly speak. All he managed to say to the man in charge of Jail number 3 was – 'Rush! Now!'

Speaking to us later assistant sub inspector of Jail number 3, V.D. Pushakarna said what he saw was beyond anything that he could have imagined. He had walked into his worst nightmare.

All the gates of the jail lay open. The jail staff which included the gatekeeper, security staff and even the duty officer Shivraj Yadav, were either sleeping or seemed to be in a daze.

Pushkarna saw that the keys to the gates of the jail were not in their usual place. The otherwise immovable, incorruptible Tamil Nadu Police sentries, chosen to guard Tihar because of the belief that their geographically distant language would stop them from fraternizing with North Indian criminals, had also been felled. Usually in their positions in tall towers around the jail, one sentry was seen lying on the road with his .303 rifle lying far away from him. Constable Prakash had covered his face not out of shame but because he too had been drugged. When he awoke from his stupor, he fell on his face, bruising it.

Pushkarna knew that something had gone terribly, terribly wrong at Tihar. So for the first time in a very long time, the buzzer (emergency alarm) was sounded for legitimate reasons, not because some ***numberdar*** wanted to take revenge on a pesky newcomer, or because they wanted to start a fight inside prison. This time, when it was sounded, it was a genuine emergency as it seemed as if the entire population of Jail number 3 had escaped.

As per routine, the ringing of the alarm bell is accompanied by the counting of the inmates. As it turned out, only 12 out of the 900 inmates who were in that particular jail had run away. But amongst those who had escaped was Tihar's most famous, Charles Gurmukh Sobhraj.

I remember very clearly where I was when I heard the news at 3 pm that day. I was watching TV at home when Doordarshan suddenly interrupted their regular programme to announce the jailbreak and that Charles Sobhraj had run away. I immediately rushed to work. On reaching, we began piecing together the sequence of events. A vital clue was the fact that each of the slumped guards was clutching a Rs 50 note. Pushkarna thus deduced that they were all first enticed with money and then given sweets laced with drugs by Charles Sobhraj on the occasion of his alleged birthday.

Needless to say, the jailbreak made headlines everywhere. A story carried by the Associated Press that was flashed all over the world quoted Delhi's Deputy Police Commissioner Ajay Aggarwal telling reporters that two men drove into Tihar and sought the warder's permission to distribute candied fruits and sweets for the birthday of one prisoner. The warder, Shivraj Yadav, granted them permission to do so and the visitors then offered sweets to him and five other guards. On consuming these sweets the jail staffers on duty passed out immediately and regained consciousness only hours later.

On investigating, we found that a former prisoner, David Hall, who had visited Sobhraj that very day, had played a key role in his escape. A British citizen, Hall had done time for smuggling drugs and had been released just a short while ago from Tihar. I did not know him well but Sobhraj did. Being foreigners at Tihar, they shared a camaraderie and their relationship was further strengthened when Sobhraj helped Hall with his bail application. On further investigation, we found records that showed that Hall had given some items to Sobhraj on the day he came to visit him – most likely ingredients which he used to drug the jail staff.

As mentioned before, unlike ordinary prisoners, Sobhraj had the privilege of cooking in his own cell and he used this to his advantage. Announcing that it was his birthday, he got sweets made in jail and slipped in a special ingredient – Larpose, a sleeping pill. According to one press report, he used 820 sleeping pills! He included 12 other prisoners in his plan – those who would never dare to escape on their own. Two of these men used to do chores for jail administration, while working in the *deodi*. They were petty criminals and claimed later that they too had been drugged by Sobhraj. When their identity was flashed in the media, they got frightened by the manhunt that had been launched for them. Before too long, the two surrendered at the Janakpuri police station and returned to Tihar. But of course the police did not want to present it as such. In a bid to restore their reputation, they announced that they had captured the two men.

But this was hardly a face-saver. As the international press swarmed to cover yet another Charles Sobhraj stunt, Delhi's top officers, along with senior government officials, rushed to Tihar. Lieutenant Governor H.K.L. Kapoor and Commissioner Ved Marwah took rounds of the jail and ordered that V.D. Pushkarna and all the other officials be arrested and interrogated. The press had gone into overdrive with stories about how Sobhraj had jail officials eating out of his hands, how he would write memos for staff members, and bribe them with large sums of money. But, the real story never came out. So, while Pushkarna was punished, the deputy superintendent of the jail, R.T.L. D'Souza was not even reprimanded. The story at the time was that D'Souza was a relative of a senior defence officer who leaned on the lieutenant governor, who was from the defence services himself.

The second story which the press at that time failed to discover was the very mysterious transfer of Charles Sobhraj from Jail number 1 to Jail number 3 just a month before his escape. Why was he moved from Jail number 1? Was it a part of the plan to escape? Jail number 3 was a relatively newer jail and so the security staff were not as well-trained as the ones in Jail number 1. Another coincidence is that around the same time this happened, David Hall, a small time drug peddler, was given bail for roughly Rs 12,000 and set free. News reports noted that while most other foreigners would have immediately headed back home, Hall hung around to come back to Tihar to help Sobhraj escape, thus indicating that a well-thought-out plan had been in place for a long time.

No one at a senior level wanted to seriously investigate Sobhraj's escape because it would have exposed their own incompetence. However, given the public outcry, they had to set up an internal inquiry led by a now defunct Frontier Service Officer. The report chose to indict Shivraj Yadav, Pushkarna and five others stating that these officials had allowed Sobhraj access to various drugs, like Larpose, and sweets. The report also alleged that their carelessness had caused all the jail staff and matrons to fall prey to Sobhraj's trap. It was all very convenient. The five were all put behind bars but later let off.

Looking back, this should not have come as a shock to any of us. During his first incarceration as a teenager in Poissy prison near Paris, Sobhraj befriended and manipulated jail officials. He was jailed in India for the first time in 1973 for an unsuccessful attempt at robbing a jewellery store at Ashoka Hotel in New Delhi. During this time he faked an illness to be admitted to a hospital, from where he escaped. In fact, Sobhraj's chosen method of poisoning dates back to the time he was arrested in Kabul between 1971 and 1972 for trying to leave without paying the bill at the Intercontinental Hotel. Again he went to the hospital by claiming to be ill, drugged the guards and escaped. This was clearly a recurring pattern with him. I am told that he drugged his murder victims before killing them as well.

But after all the *tamasha*, 23 days later, Charles Sobhraj came back to Tihar. He had been arrested in Goa. What gave him away was a runaway, Ajay Singh Tomar, who was detained in Mumbai (then Bombay) for trying to board a train with a bag carrying a live grenade and cartridges. Tomar then led the police to a hotel where they nabbed another escaped convict, Devkumar Brahmadutt Tyagi. After questioning, the duo told the police that Sobhraj and Hall had split from them and left for Goa. Sobhraj and Hall were finally arrested in Goa. Police recovered a gun from Sobhraj and cash worth US $12,000 from Hall. Apparently the latter had arranged it for them to be used as getaway money.

Sobhraj's arrest was extremely stressful for some Tihar jail staff members. As the police interrogated him, trying to get to the bottom of the jailbreak conspiracy, they all held their breath. Would Sobhraj give them away? Would he name all those he had on his payroll? There were so many rumours about Sobhraj at the time. Apparently he had a dictaphone strapped to his knee at all times to record the superintendent and the deputy superintendent asking for bribes. With so much scrutiny about his escape, would that open secret finally be out? But there was no need for such concern because nothing changes, even when there are such big exposés.

When I met him soon after he returned to Tihar in April 1986,

I asked him why he had run away. It was during my night shift and so I had some time to kill. He simply smiled and said, 'I like creating a sensation.' The press, however, reported that he had orchestrated the jailbreak because he wanted to be arrested. This was because his jail time in India was almost done and he was due to be extradited to Thailand where he would have faced the firing squad for the multiple murders he had committed. The jailbreak gave the Indian authorities an added reason to keep him longer.

Having said that, I do believe Sobhraj – he wanted to create a sensation. He wanted to be the only high-profile prisoner to have beaten the jail security multiple times. Of course, all this grandstanding was only for my benefit. In court, he had to deny everything. His submission was that he had been kidnapped by intelligence agencies who wanted to extract information from him, and therefore it was he who was a victim. He told me at some point too, that the jailbreak was actually a conspiracy. Knowing just how elaborately he had planned and pretended to have a birthday party, I laughed. 'Be serious,' he responded sternly.

Contrary to this , the police had a different theory. They blamed another high-profile inmate and Sobhraj's cellmate, Rajendra Sethia, a prominent Delhi businessman. The prosecutors at that time alleged that Sethia had hired Sobhraj to 'liquidate' a key witness in the bank scam that he was accused in. The witness was a certain Swami Satsangi and in order to get him killed, Sethia had allegedly asked Sobhraj for help. In return, Sethia's wife apparently deposited $99,000 in a UK account and police claim, there was a withdrawal from it just before Sobhraj's escape. The police theory was completely denied and Sethia went to the court to get it quashed.

Despite his influential friends and compromised officials, Charles Sobhraj could not escape the grim reality that was waiting for him when he was brought back to Tihar. He had to pay for the humiliation we had to endure because of his antics. From complete freedom of movement, he was now kept in a segregated ward and in fetters. Kept in a high-security ward meant for terrorists, his movements were under surveillance around the clock and he was not allowed to go anywhere without a security guard.

But Charles Sobhraj used a loophole that all clever inmates use to get away from the drudgery, heat and loneliness of jail life. They make the most of court visits. In court, you can meet outsiders, family members and maybe even get decent food. An *India Today* report from September 1986 describes these early days and how Sobhraj would find reprieve in his courtroom appearances:

> He obviously wants to prolong his stay in court – in jail he has to wear fetters all the time. After the main arguments are over, he interjects with three requests calculated to prolong the proceedings. With the confidence born of experience, he seeks the permission of the court to have food in judicial custody, an interview with his counsel Sneh Sengar and permission to inspect the files. Permissions obtained, he has ample time to socialize.
>
> Oozing his famous "bikini-killer" charm, he walks across the courtroom to kiss Rajendra Sethia's wife and sister, who have come to meet Sethia. After exchanging pleasantries, Sobhraj turns his attention to the chicken biryani brought for him in a polythene bag while an angry Sneh Sengar argues heatedly with him. Calmly, Sobhraj pacifies Sengar with a few words while absentmindedly toying with the neck of the chicken. As a constable gruffly reminds him of the forgotten food he shoos him away. Another man hovering around is sent off for a Limca.

I remember the bizarre twist behind his new fettered existence. We wanted to put him in chains but the Indian legal system was very clear that the jail superintendent's wish to do so was not enough. There had to be a legitimate court direction. This was very tricky because physically shackling a man can be seen as being amongst the worst human rights violations. No district judge wanted to put his name on such an order. At least three months went by and then finally, there was a new district and sessions judge called P.K. Bahri.

Justice Bahri, who eventually retired as a high court judge went the other extreme. Not only did he quickly approve of shackling Sobhraj, he also did it in haste. His order was flawed as it implied that Sobhraj could be kept in fetters indefinitely. As a law officer, I knew that the maximum time you could put someone in chains was for three months. Obviously, Judge Bahri was what we like to call a 'bold judicial officer'. That's the thing about our judicial system, it has all the provisions of being liberal and visionary but you can break the best of these systems if you know whom to approach. So, if you had a terrorist in your hands in the '80s and you did not want to deal with all this human rights mumbo-jumbo then you went and saw Judge Bahri (or an equally 'bold' judge). Unlike other judges, he did not care about the consequences or the optics.

Sobhraj was now literally a chained version of his former self, constantly under watch. Even then, from time to time, he would surprise us. For instance, when he was in the segregation ward, a small amount of hash was discovered in between slices of bread. It was beyond us to decipher how someone was able to sneak in drugs in such a high-security area. Two constables were suspended and later sacked for supplying drugs to Sobhraj. Perhaps, even a case was filed against them. But how could you punish a man who was already in the darkest section of Tihar and had heavy iron shackles around his ankles?

Sobhraj also became the reason a number of people lost their jobs, and not just those from the lower rungs. Before he was eventually released to leave India for France in 1997, he also became the prime cause for star police officer Kiran Bedi's transfer. When Inspector General Kiran Bedi, was posted to oversee 8,000 inmates of Tihar in 1993, it had been years since his jailbreak, and the fetters were now forgotten. Kiran Bedi's downfall was that she spotted the same talent in him that we all did. All prisoners are meant to do some work and so Madam Bedi stationed him in the legal aid cell where he was given a typewriter. According to jail rules, it is up to the jail in charge to decide who gets a typewriter. There was nothing illegal about it. But by this time the then Delhi Chief Minister Madan Lal Khurana was just looking for an excuse to punish Kiran Bedi and he found that excuse in Sobhraj. Her transfer order made out that the typewriter was an item of indulgence and luxury and that it was helping Sobhraj write bestseller books glorifying his own exploits. Citing this as the reason, Magsayay award winner Kiran Bedi was removed from Tihar. Archaic jail rules were used to punish the person who had carried out the most dramatic prison reforms in the country.

Once Sobhraj's 20-year-jail term ended on 17 February 1997, he was handed over to the French authorities. At that time, he was 53 years old. There were still some pending cases but the government decided that it was better to release him since France said they would take him back. Sobhraj enjoyed freedom in Paris for a few years but was again arrested in Nepal in 2003 and has been serving out a life sentence ever since.

~

Having spent about four decades in Tihar, I can safely say that Tihar is a trendsetter as far as jailbreaks go. The modus operandi adopted by those who have escaped from Tihar was copied by others in various prisons. And this predates Charles Sobhraj and his daring jailbreak.

One such legendary escape took place in 1976 much before I joined Tihar. It was during the Emergency when many opposition leaders were jailed by Prime Minister Indira Gandhi under the Maintenance of Internal Security Act (MISA). Tihar housed the likes of Vijaya Raje Scindia, Nanaji Deshmukh, Chaudhary Charan Singh, George Fernandes, Arun Jaitley, Prakash Singh Badal, Lala Hansraj and Prem Sagar Gupta at the time. Vijaya Raje Scindia and Nanaji Deshmukh were from the Jan Sangh, while George Fernandes, a trade union leader, was from the Socialist Party.

Since the facilities were overcrowded, new cells were created appropriating the open area to make comfortable spaces for the high-profile inmates. The hospital extension was nearby if any of them needed medical attention. Jail staffers witnessed history as Nanaji Deshmukh and others initiated talks with the Communists and the Janata Party was created in Tihar Jail.

Vijaya Raje Scindia had a key role in the formation of the party. Housed in Ward 3 she had to find a way to meet Nanaji Deshmukh, who was in Ward 18. She knew that he was an expert in yoga and so she had a doctor write a prescription that ordered her to do yoga for an hour every day. The jail staff had no choice. They allowed Deshmukh to go across to the women's ward every day to teach the Rajmata yoga. I am not sure how much yoga they did, but these deliberations were the seed of the Janata Party.

When these leaders were not plotting to overthrow Indira Gandhi, they used to take part in other activities to fight the boredom of prison. Arun Jaitley played badminton with the jail staff, George Fernandes wrote a lot and Chaudhary Charan Singh, who was of a more religious bent of mind, would conduct *havans*. Prakash Singh Badal was a link between the Jan Sangh leaders and the Communists and brought them together. They would talk politics and play carrom. In all this excitement, sensing an opportunity, 13 men serving life sentences dug a tunnel through their barracks and escaped from Tihar on 16 March 1976, exactly a decade before Sobhraj. Most of them were caught but many of them were also released later by the Sentence Review Board. The board which exists till this day is empowered to decide on applications of early release. Many convicts who feel they are reformed, have been on good behaviour in prison qualify for release and are given that option. Jessica Lal's killer Manu Sharma has been trying for years to get an early release and failed but the 'Tandoor killer' Sushil Sharma was successful with the board after serving more than two decades in prison.

~

The first big jail break that happened during my time at Tihar took place in the summer of 1983 and involved students of Jawaharlal Nehru University (JNU). It all started with a student agitation against the then JNU Vice Chancellor P.N. Shrivastava, who had ordered the hostel transfer of a student because of a disciplinary issue, leading to the entire student body surrounding the teachers. Between April and May, things deteriorated with the students cutting off the power and phone connections of the vice chancellor and rector, leading to the 10 May events when the police entered the campus and arrested 250 students for arson and rioting. In total, 170 male students and 80 female students were arrested and kept in separate jails.

It seemed like a routine matter until the day after i.e. 11 May, when in the lock-out count, 55 female students and 125 male students were missing. All hell broke loose. Unable to handle the stress, the deputy superintendent of jails, M.S. Ritu, went on leave citing his wife's ill health as a reason. He did not even sign off on closing the jail down (a protocol that is followed in times of an emergency, which this clearly was!) because he would have been held responsible. That job fell on his deputy, Shivraj Yadav (the same person who was punished later for the Sobhraj breakout).

The news of the escape soon reached the media. A fresh FIR had to be lodged against the students. The investigators reached JNU armed with warrants against those that had gone missing from jail. But to their surprise they found that the names did not match the students staying there. They had all given fictitious names on arrest! The police then realized the huge loophole that existed in the system – anyone could give a fictitious name because there was no verification process in place.

We still did not know how 180 students had gone missing despite being in a high-security prison. It was actually a combination of our vulnerable system and the students' ingenuity. As students, they were classified as B-Class inmates or elite group of prisoners, which meant they were allowed to meet visitors without any physical barriers between them such as glass walls or iron bars.

Many of the students were children of influential people and had a large number of visitors on the first day they were brought to Tihar. The practice at that time was that all visitors were stamped on their wrists and this stamp was checked when they left the prison gates to ensure that it was indeed a visitor who was leaving. Bear in mind, this was the month of May, the peak of Delhi summer. The clever students took advantage of the fact the stamp was easily transferable on to another wrist thanks to the heat and sweat. The visitors used their stamps to stamp the wrists of the students and out walked 180 students, never to be traced again. It is another matter that if the gatekeeper had been vigilant, he would have noticed that the number of people leaving Tihar was nearly thrice the number of visitors who had entered! I am told that many of those JNU students are now top bureaucrats themselves. One of them even went on to become the jail superintendent of Tihar!

With each such incident, hard lessons were learnt. After this one, prisoners could no longer meet visitors face to face or in their wards. But the escapes did not stop. In fact, some of them were hilarious.

In 1988, a jailbreak occurred as the result of an old habit of our jailers to get massages from prisoners in the afternoon. Deputy Superintendent L.P. Nirmal liked to get one every afternoon and would often doze off in the middle of the massage. One of his appointed masseurs decided that this was too good an opportunity to miss. So, as soon as he lulled Nirmal to sleep with his magic fingers, he noted that he could easily change into the uniform that the officer had removed while getting a massage. Dressed as L.P. Nirmal, the inmate walked out of the front gate of Tihar after taking a salute from the jail officers. It shows just how disinterested everyone at Tihar really was, they did not even recognize their own boss. They just saw someone wearing a uniform with two stars on his shoulders and they saluted him. Of course, we caught him soon after because he had not gone too far. He was found napping at his sister's house, still wearing L.P. Nirmal's uniform.

On another occasion a drug addict tried to escape. When a drug addict has withdrawal symptoms, he is so desperate he can do anything. Apparently, this person was in that state when he jumped off the Jail number 3 wall in the middle of the night. Jail number 1, 2 and 3 are interconnected so if you jump from one, you land in the other, but in his current state of mind, this inmate thought he was already outside. He asked the guard standing there where the bus stop was, which ensured that his freedom was extremely short-lived.

In 2015, two boys jumped off the wall of Jail number 5, into another jail complex. Realizing that jumping off the second jail's wall was not feasible, they decided to dig a hole in the wall, and it worked. There have been many cases of inmates escaping with service workers like with Public Works Department (PWD) labourers who come to Tihar for daily labour work.

Other than Sobhraj's escape, the one that embarrassed Tihar the most was the escape of the Bandit Queen and Member of Parliament Phoolan Devi's killer Sher Singh Rana in February 2004. When a prisoner was to appear in a court in another town, the state police was engaged to transport them and not Tihar staff who are familiar with the inmates. The logic behind this was that since the state police would be more familiar with local routes, they would be able to navigate the roads more efficiently. The transit requests would be done by wireless sets and this was a loophole just waiting to be exploited.

On 5 February 2004, soon after a wireless message was received a team arrived to take Sher Singh Rana to a court in Haridwar. According to the system, we gave the security men 'diet money' – an allowance for meals along the journey, and handed him over along with his warrant and other documents. Sometime later, another police team appeared. That was when the penny dropped. We had handed over Rana not to a police team, but to a well-coordinated escape team. We had not even properly checked the credentials of the 'police' team that came to collect Rana. They did not have a copy of the official communication that had been sent from us but we had let it pass because they claimed any delay would upset the court. And that was enough for us to hand over Rana immediately. That is the root of the problem – the jail staff are so scared about being hauled up by courts, that they will do anything to avoid any trouble.

But the system soon changed. Instead of a state police team, Delhi police began escorting prisoners for out of town appearances. For once, it appeared that a senior officer was going to lose his job over Rana's escape. Director General Ajay Aggarwal was admonished by the Delhi Lieutenant Governor Vijai Kapoor and threatened with departmental action. But yet again he remained untouched while his juniors lost their jobs. It has always been that way, senior officers are never held responsible.

If you look at the last prison data that was released by the National Crime Records Bureau in 2016, it shows that escapes are still much less from jails and usually happen en route to court appearances. Delhi, for instance, had only one case of escape in 2016 from Tihar Jail. There were 89 jail breaks across the country but 272 inmates were able to escape while they were being taken to court or to hospital for checkups or just from police custody. Do you how many were re-arrested? Only 34 per cent.

LONELINESS OF A JAILER

1986 was not only marked by Charles Sobhraj's jailbreak. It was also the year I met Poonam, my wife of more than three decades. Tihar brought us together but it is not an exaggeration to say that Tihar also almost tore us apart.

In fact, looking back now, it is a wonder that I found a companion while working in Tihar. I almost did not and if I had listened to my family, there was a good chance that I may have spent my life cursing my miserable existence there. In their eyes, I was well educated with a government job, from a respectable family that owned land and a valuable 'property' in the Capital – a suitable boy personified. The reality, however, was very different.

My job was driving away prospective brides. I believed I would have a long line of women vying to 'land' me but while I rejected some women, many of them dismissed me outright soon after they asked, 'What does he do?' Others were concerned about my working hours when I would tell them that I would only come home late, around 11 pm, after having done the releases for the evening.

Jailers in those days had a sordid reputation. We were considered highly corrupt. In fact, I would go so far as to say that in the public's opinion, the staff in Tihar was as criminal as those who were locked up there. This may explain why at the age of 32, I was still a bachelor.

A common friend introduced me to Poonam and by some stroke of luck, she was not entirely repulsed by my job. Perhaps she was sensitized because she lived just a block away from Tihar. She was a school teacher who would finish work at 2 pm and that was downtime for me at work. Some of my colleagues took naps during this time, but I took advantage of this time to get to know her better. I would pick her up from school and we would go to restaurants or I would just go and spend time with her at her home. I wanted her to get to know my work well and why I did what I did. Even then, I realized that she would have to make a psychological adjustment to live inside the jail complex and I wanted to give her as much time as possible to be sure of her decision. Otherwise, how else would she understand the strange ways of my colleagues, the paranoia that made our workplace such a toxic environment, the strange kind of inferiority complex we nursed that stemmed from the status attached to our jobs. To give one example, while we wore khaki and were expected to work like the police, we were not the police and we certainly were not paid like them. But we were not civilians either and had tough jobs that demanded we enforce the law just like cops did. However, we did not command the same respect or get the perks the police did. It made us angry because after all, one reason we were drawn to the job was to be a part of a uniformed force.

The government said we could not get paid the same as the police because we were civilians and did not work as hard. But they didn't even pay us like other bureaucrats. We were as they say in Hindi, '*na ghar ka na ghat ka*' (neither here nor there). Policemen also looked down upon us and we took it very badly. And yet, the police force's bad reputation stuck with us too. That was the reason even my brother and sister faced difficulty getting married. If a potential match was found, their family would point out, 'Their brother is in the police. If something goes wrong between the husband and wife, he will put them in jail!' If only they knew just how powerless the jail staff really is. We were so low in the pecking order that there was a good chance we would even be bullied by the inmates, that is, if we survived our boss's tyranny. The choice was simple. Either you gave into the demands that rich, powerful inmates made of you and became their corrupt crony, or you risked being beaten up and constantly threatened.

To do such a job requires immense mental and physical strength. That was the reason why my jail colleagues were unimpressed when they saw my frail physique. 'Sir, you look very weak,' they said to me. I could not figure out why until I realized that it was common for us to get physically assaulted by inmates. In fact, some jail officers have even been killed by inmates. Imagine a scenario where an influential inmate demands something outside of the rules and you as a jailer put your foot down. It is not so easy because there are consequences for turning down these demands. No wonder, corruption just seems like an easier option – you survive until you retire and earn your provident fund. If you are lucky and do not receive threats or beatings, you get transferred. So, when my colleagues sized up my 56 kg frame, they took me to be one of the submissive ones – the kind who would play along and then run at the hint of any trouble.

If this was not enough, what made my case worse was the fact that I was also a Gupta and if you ask why this is relevant, you are perhaps forgetting the story of my first day in Tihar. One of the key reasons why Vij told me to buzz off and that he had no vacancy despite me having an offer letter was because he didn't want someone from my caste around. He wanted someone from his home state of Haryana.

Some of you may think that India has moved on and we have all these anti-discrimination laws in place, but if you look around, you will find that we are still identified by our caste. So if you were a 'Gujjar', 'Meena', 'Thakur' or 'Jat', then you were thought to be strict and powerful because you belonged to the warrior caste. When inmates would hear my name, they would say, 'Oh, he is a *baniya*' or 'Oh, he is a Gupta', 'How can he tackle us? We will deal with him.' I had the misfortune of being from a community that had a long, glorious historical tradition of being less than brave. I don't know about other workplaces but in my case, casteism was alive and thriving. While the Meenas or Jats had existing officers to protect new recruits who belonged to their community, I had no other Gupta or *baniya* to defend me. So my name and my appearance led me to being threatened both by my colleagues and the prisoners. At some point I stopped using my full name and would sign all letters 'Sunil Kumar'. But even this did not work because by now everyone knew I was a *baniya*. I was determined to work twice as hard to establish that I was not a pushover, but the stereotype did not leave me. So I had to resort to other tactics...

~

Sobhraj's gang of villainous jail terrorizers had rich, influential criminals such as Sunil Batra, Vipin Jaggi, Ravi Kapoor and Prem Shankar Shukla. Batra and Jaggi were in prison because they were part of a big Union Bank robbery in 1970. The two of them had got the death penalty for robbing the bank's van of the six lakh rupees it was carrying and shooting and killing the driver and the guard of the bank. The death sentence was later commuted to life imprisonment during which time Batra and Jaggi along with the others in the group became a menace to other prisoners. They would roam around the jail complex looking for someone to extort by either arm twisting or thrashing them. Because they were rich, they had no fear of the law as they had many lawyers who negotiated their way through the courts. In fact, many of them were forever in court filing one application after another against officials they did not like (another intimidation tactic).

But while Batra and Jaggi were to be feared, Prem Shankar Shukla was in another league altogether. In fact, Shukla was so brazen that he once went to a police station that was handling a fraud case against him, dressed as a DIG. He told them he wanted to inspect the files. Seeing he was a senior official, they readily agreed and gave him full access. Before they knew what was happening, Shukla disappeared with his own case file! I came face to face with him when we both had to go to Supreme Court. Shukla had to appear in front of the court and I was the official presenting his case. In the courtroom, I saw that Shukla was sitting up front with lawyers and the guard who was meant to be keeping him in check was relegated to the back of the room. I was shocked to see Shukla's behaviour and immediately called the guard and asked him why had he allowed him to roam around freely. Admonished, the guard walked up to Shukla and pointed at me. Shukla looked towards me and I heard him say, 'I don't know who he is.'

I was furious. The cheek of that bloody criminal! I wanted Shukla to regret his behaviour. As soon as we got back to Tihar, I summoned the *munshi* and told him to give Shukla a beating to remember. The order was duly noted, and from the *munshi* it was passed on to the *numberdar*. However, it was not so simple. Shukla would definitely approach the courts or any other influential person he knew, so the beating had to be planned in such a way that it looked like the inmates were fighting amongst themselves. In this, I managed to succeed and as soon as it was done, I summoned Shukla and the ones he was allegedly fighting with. I noticed, to my satisfaction, that he had a few scrapes on his body. I immediately called the police because that was the standard operating procedure. Shukla, being no novice, also knew the game. When the police asked him what happened, he did not blame any of us and played down the entire incident. 'Nothing happened, we were just messing around,' he said.

But as I had anticipated, Shukla did prepare a petition for the high court. I was ready too – I presented his statement to the police where he stated that no one was responsible for his injuries. It was then that Shukla realized that he had met his match. Later, when his wounds had healed, he asked me,'Why did you have me beaten up?'

'*Beta*, I am a jailer, I am your *baap*. So don't act smart, telling people that you don't know who I am.'

'Don't worry sir, I won't be in Tihar too long.'

True to his word, he soon got himself transferred to another jail. I would like to believe that I had established myself as the terror in Tihar, but the truth is that I had a lifetime of battles to fight and Prem Shankar Shukla was nothing compared to the adversaries I would face in the times to come.

~

My first struggle though was personal. From 1986 to 1988, I tried to slowly ease Poonam into this jungle. I would regale her with tales of my own challenges, the strange beings that played such an important part of my day and hoped that she would become the one bright spark in it. She had to get used to the idea that we were not going to be living in a community of civilized, genial folks. The jail officers may be aspiring for parity with the police force, but there were so many jailers who worked at Tihar who were basically illiterate. I am not exaggerating. The minimum educational qualification for a jail guard's job was only introduced in 1986 when they said he or she had to be a matriculate pass. Before that many of them who had served as servers (peons) to the superintendent would be recruited to this position. As I said earlier each mishap or jailbreak in Tihar led to a huge learning experience or reforms being put in place. This reworking of 'Recruitment Rules' or 'RR' as we called it was a direct result of Sobhraj's escape.

However, I must add that the revolution was not completely effective. According to me only 40 per cent of those who work in jails are fully trained or are competent enough to do their jobs. Looking back, even my offer letter and appointment could be deemed 'illegal'. Only someone at the level of a director general or an inspector general could make appointments at the level that I joined. The superintendent was king and he did whatever he pleased, gave offer letters to whoever he liked and sent others packing. Maybe this is why so many in Tihar questioned why I had joined them in the first place. With my law degree, could I not have done something better with my life? All this education to come and work in this jungle?

What I did not share with anyone (not even Poonam) was that I had a romantic idea of our work. An idea, that went beyond official positions, seniority, corruption and violence. I aspired for something higher and thought of our work as similar to that of housekeeping. We had to run Tihar as someone would run his house. We would take care of bedding, food, rations, clothing, and sometimes, just sometimes, we would take care of the minds of those who lived here. I wished for the days in which jailers were respected and people had a positive image of them. Like in the classic film *Khaan Dost,* where the hero Raj Kapoor plays a jail official. He is shown to be so upright and honest that he can't figure out how to manage the 5,000 rupees that he needs for his sister's wedding. But I was confronted by a reality that was totally different. We had a powerful opportunity to reform minds but were caught up in petty issues. Who cared if Tamil Nadu police had the job of searching you as you entered, that CRPF ran the scanners and X-Ray machines and the Tamil Nadu Special Police or (TSP) were jointly in charge of the high-security ward? Why did we feel envious that we were not entrusted to do all this? We had the job of being judicial custodians which could be so rewarding.

Just when I felt Poonam was getting to understand me, and the life I had chosen, my parents threw me a googly. They did not think Poonam was the right match for me. Apparently, because she was too short! I am almost six feet tall and she is an entire foot shorter than me, so they felt we would not look good together, not realizing that it was actually me who had fallen short of 'ratings' in the marriage market.

If only they knew about my colleagues' struggle to find a suitable spouse. Those in demanding professions such as medicine marry from within the fraternity because it is easier to understand each other's circumstances. But in ours, we would never do that because the other person would just remind us of our despair filled existence, and they would know how we work in sub-standard condition.

A male jailer marrying a female one is very rare. In fact, things are so bad that some women staffers have even married convicts. Examples of colleagues marrying late and making compromises were all around me. Like Matron Raju Mukherjee who married a convicted rapist.

This incident goes back to the time when the women's section was inside the jail in the '80s. What is currently divided as Jail number 1, 2 and 3 was at that time a single unit that also housed a women's section. Today the complete segregation of male and female staff means they do not even cross each other's paths, but back then it was different. Matron Raju Mukherjee would walk through the common areas to reach the women's quarters where her job was to do the lock-in for the evening. I remember very clearly that she was beautiful, in fact, very beautiful. An orderly of the deputy superintendent of the jail who was serving out the regular seven-year sentence for committing rape would chat to her every day. They eventually got married when he finished his sentence and was released.

Now when I think back, there was not much fuss about the whole thing. Of course our jail manual forbids any kind of 'familiarity' between a staff member and an inmate: 'no subordinate officer shall correspond, or hold any intercourse whatever with any discharged prisoner, or allow them to visit or remain in their quarters.' Forget marriage, it said you shouldn't even, 'Treat any prisoner with familiarity.'

However, no one wanted to take any action against Matron Raju Mukherjee. She was an orphan who grew up in Nari Niketan and had no family of her own. So perhaps people were happy for her and did not let it become a huge scandal. Maybe things would have been different if she was a high-ranking official. The orderly's prison sentence was commuted on the basis of his good behaviour and I am told they are still quite happy together.

There were other stories of higher-level officers marrying prisoners. There was one case that involved a lady doctor. Jail rules allowed female doctors to treat male patients although rules did not allow the reverse (unless of course, they needed a specialist in which special allowances were made). One particular lady doctor, who was a homeopath doctor, fancied an inmate and they eventually got married.

A similar case involved Gurdeep Bagga or Pinki as he was popularly known. Bagga had been in Tihar since 1980 serving out a life sentence for murder. He was a really good looking young man from a decent family that lived in the tony neighbourhood of Hauz Khas in Delhi. I knew about his family because his sisters often came to visit him in jail, which was most unusual. If a prisoner belonged to a low-income family that lived in harsh circumstances, his family members were too busy surviving and had little time to visit him. But, Bagga's family, especially the women, would always come to see him.

In jail you quickly get to know the 'good guys' from the 'bad guys'. I could tell that Bagga was in jail because he had been at the wrong place at the wrong time. He was in a hurry to get a gas cylinder but the shop manager engaged him in a fight, resulting in Bagga stabbing him. It was a dispute that went out of control. Not just me, even the Delhi High Court felt bad that an otherwise seemingly decent guy lost his cool. The Delhi High Court's judgement read,

> The act is completely out of utter desperation while deprived of self-control. The appellant is a young man with a good background. He has no criminal history. We strongly feel that this young life should not pass within the four walls of jail. We make a recommendation to the government to exercise its powers of reprieve and substantially remit or commute the sentence.

The woman who fell in love with Bagga was my own intern. She was in her early twenties, doing master's in social work and came to work with me through a common contact. One day, when I came back from court, I saw the two of them in my room. She was doing a research project on prison methodology and had been there for about a month. I could sense that there was something going on between the two. I suppose they both came from educated backgrounds and just hit it off. By a double stroke of luck he got a reduction in his life sentence and found someone who wanted to marry him despite his time in jail. As I said, Bagga's lack of criminal intention and good behaviour in jail earned him the early release. There would be no shame or judgement about this period in his life, because they had met and love had blossomed in the unlikeliest place – in prison itself! In my entire career I have never seen the president commute anyone's sentence in the way Bagga's was from life imprisonment to 10 years.

In 1987, soon after Bagga was released and my intern left her position, the two got married. I was invited for their wedding but I did not go because I have a policy of not accepting any invitations from inmates. Of course, years later I did accept his Facebook friend request. I saw that he has done well for himself – he runs a distillery business in various parts of the world and travels extensively. I am told his marriage is still strong and I am happy for them.

In all these relationships that were born inside Tihar, I was also concerned about whether they would last because many inmates have low self esteem. I was especially concerned that Matron Raju Mukherjee's – former convict – husband would leave her. But I am happy to be proved wrong in that case too.

Part of the reason behind this phenomenon, which you will accept as being not too rare by the number of examples I have given, is a movie that came out in 1983. In the hugely successful movie, *Hero*, starring Jackie Shroff and Meenakshi Seshadri, the main protagonist is a guy who is in jail. I think it became trendy and somewhat acceptable to marry someone who had a prison record. That's true at least in Bagga's case.

However, most women in jail were resigned to the fact that they could not be acceptable to men with the kind of jobs they held. When I joined Tihar, there were four women prison guards and I remember them as being quite old, either single or divorced – none of them had a good family life. However, today things are different where we have very good talent amongst us. Educated women are joining the team every day and from totally illiterate staff, we have gone on to have PhDs, BTechs and MTechs.

~

There is a joke that all of us in the jail service like to tell each other. There was a jailer who was very religious. He was so into God that he would pray all day, every day. Impressed with his devotion, God appeared and said, 'Ask for whatever you want but there is one condition.' The jailer asked 'What?' 'You can have anything you want but the condition is that your neighbour will receive double of whatever that is.' The jailer was in a real spot. What the hell? Why did his neighbour have to get double of what he got? So he thought and thought and then he finally knew what he should ask God for. 'You can blind me in one eye.'

We would laugh every time we told someone new this story but imagine the pathetic reality. Our petty insecurities manifested into such torturous levels that it led to us becoming sadistic creatures. Like in the joke, we do not gain happiness from good things happening to us as much as we got satisfaction hearing of others' misfortunes. We just could not stand the idea of anything good happening to a colleague. I am not just saying this frivolously. There was a nationwide survey that was done which asked us if jail staff would like to be promoted to supervisors or would they prefer people from outside services. An overwhelming number of them voted to say that they did not want to be promoted; they wanted outsiders to come and boss them around. Can you imagine that? It means accepting the possibility that you will never really get to rise to a senior position. That is why if you look up our records, there has perhaps been only one person who has actually risen up from our services, the rest are all from other cadres. They come from state cadres, quietly do their work knowing they are only going to be here for a few years and without trying to change anything too much.

Of course, not all of it was because of the hate-thy-neighbour-syndrome. Some of it was also carefully thought out. Say one of us did become the supervisor we would know exactly why certain things didn't work, how corruption happened, how jailbreaks happened. We could perhaps overlook it once or twice but we could not allow the kind of rot to continue, could we? So at some point, we would have to take action. But if you had a superintendent from outside, they would have no clue about our ways. If they were greedy, the other officials would give him a cut. Otherwise, most of them were just happy to be left alone.

~

Having spent two years on her orientation or what other couples would refer to as 'dating', Poonam and I got married in April 1988. We first lived in Sainik Vihar but I decided to move into the jail complex because my working hours were too demanding. Mine was almost a 24-hour job. I would start my day at 6 am when I opened the jail and counted the prisoners. Between 1 and 3 pm, I could go back home and rest and come back only to release the prisoners, which meant that I was occupied with duties until 10 pm. Before my wife complained about this schedule, someone else did – my brother's wife.

Her source of frustration was that my ageing and ill parents were being looked after solely by my brother. 'Why can't Sunil do it instead?' she would often and perhaps, very reasonably, ask. My brother (God bless him!), would tell her off and point out that my job just did not allow me to do these domestic duties. I do not know about my sister-in-law but I don't think my parents ever understood this either. I think it is fair to say that I neglected them in the end. They would stay alone at home with just a helper to do their errands. And while I assuaged my guilt of having provided for them, I knew that without our supervision, the helper would not care for them well.

If my brother's family and parents were unhappy, so was Poonam. 'If I knew about your work timings before, I would have never married you,' she often said. This became a common refrain at home. She really meant it too, I think. Life happened to us – we had a daughter and soon after a son but our fighting did not stop. She found a new reason to harangue me, 'I am bringing up the kids, what are you doing?' Marriage is a tough adjustment for every couple but I know that I brought so much extra baggage with my job that calling it challenging would be an understatement. It was so tough at times I even gave her notice for divorce. Why? Because I wanted to work with my conscience intact but my wife would compare us with others. 'Why do they have this?', 'Why do they have that?', 'Why don't we have anything?'

I always had a car but she wouldn't be happy and always point to my colleague's car which would be flashier. I would tell her 'Why do you care? He is living off what he has earned and so are we. Why do you look at them? I have what I work for, you have what you earn, and they will pay the price for what they have.' Nobody seemed impressed with the fact that I took a high moral position and no favours from any prisoners.

I could not get Poonam the fancier car, but I did change one thing. In 1996, I accepted the position of being a law officer for Tihar. By that time, I was having daily run-ins with my colleagues and as Poonam complained, I was always the submissive party. When I got a promotion and became senior deputy superintendent, I knew that the jail staff just would not let me do my job. I knew about their smack supply chains, their extortion rackets and if I dared to disrupt it, they would launch their artillery against me. Instead of saying 'bring it on', I chose the peaceful life. The new position meant I would go to work at a more respectable time of 9 am, look after the various court appearances and the questions that the court was asking of Tihar Jail, and then soon after the courts closed, I could go home. I would still live in the jail complex. If a prisoner ran away, he could still jump over the wall and land in my backyard, but after 15 years, I was opting out of the lock-in and lock-out of prison duties. My power was a little less in this job but frankly, I thought it was a very small price to pay. I was free to go home at six every evening and for the first time, my weekends were really mine.

I wanted to minimize the influence jails had on my children. The walls of our bungalow and that of the jail were lined together but till date, no one from my family has even peeped in to see what Tihar looks like from the inside. I know in Telangana, they have made a tourist spot out of their jails and encourage people to come and visit them for a fee. But I do not like the idea at all. Jails are not zoos which people visit. I saw too many questionable influences seeping in through the walls and into our lives. I tried to bring up Himani and Angad, my daughter and son, differently but I could not deny that the children in our colony were different. If you walk down a neighbourhood, you may find children greeting you with a 'namaste uncle' or 'hello'. This would never happen in ours. Maybe, it was because we were in such close proximity of perceived evil, there was always fear in their hearts. My children had this recurring nightmare that prisoners would dig their way out of jail and the tunnel would lead right inside our house. That's probably because when 13 prisoners dug their way out of Tihar in 1976, the tunnel did open inside our colony. They were afraid of jail riots or when TV crews came to interview me, they got scared that I was a marked man for angry, vengeful prisoners.

There were no dearth of nightmares but I think my children turned out okay. Himani got a degree in bio-technology and works for a multinational company. She recently got married to a very nice boy (and I was very happy that my career had not been a factor in their marriage at all). Angad is an IT engineer and has a good, well-earning job. Poonam still works at the private school and yes, she still says she would not have married me if she knew the kind of life she was going to lead. It makes me laugh but it is fair to say that our over three decades of marriage have not been smooth, we have had to struggle it out every single day. Although, if I am ever to receive the President's medal for distinguished service, I would share it with Poonam for she has been with me every step of the way.

THE CRIME THAT CHANGED DELHI FOREVER

Less than two years after I joined Tihar, I saw two men being hanged to death in front of my eyes. I knew this day was inevitable and maybe it is monstrous of me to say, but I was both disturbed and excited to witness my first execution. Until that day, I had only seen hangings in movies and read about them in books and the idea that I was going to be part of such a moment was overwhelming. It was baffling to my mind that a living, breathing person who I had been talking to would cease existing so suddenly. But this was a reality I had to accept quickly and in this regard the system helped play a part. At least a week before the execution, the entire prison machinery kicked in with manuals, court orders and step-by-step instructions to tell us what to do, which somewhat normalized the process of ending someone's life. We followed each one of those rules that had been laid down in the nineteenth century (some even older) and some oral hand-me-down instructions to hang Billa and Ranga, the rapist and murderer duo. This was the case that changed Delhi forever.

On 26 August 1978, two teenagers who had hitchhiked a ride early evening were kidnapped, raped and murdered in the heart of the Capital. This was the crime that Billa and Ranga had been tried and convicted of and it was this case that would prep me for the role of the 'accidental' hangman that I would eventually become. But I am getting ahead of myself. We followed the jail manual word for word to implement the Supreme Court's order that stated Billa and Ranga 'are professional murderers and deserve no sympathy' and that by their 'elimination the society would be much better of'. Nothing possibly could or should go wrong. But something did go wrong. Something really big.

~

It was after 6 pm on that fateful day that Geeta Chopra left her home at the Service Officers' Enclave, Dhaula Kuan along with her brother Sanjay. She had to host a show on All India Radio and Sanjay was to be on the show too. Sixteen-year-old Geeta was a student at Jesus and Mary College while 14-year-old Sanjay studied at Modern School. The radio show *Yuva Vani* aired at 8 pm post which their father, Indian Navy Captain Madan Mohan Chopra, was to pick them up from Akashwani Bhawan at 9 pm. When the Chopras tuned into the radio at 8 pm, they did not hear their teenage daughter's voice but someone else's. They thought, perhaps, the show timing had changed or they just had the radio station mixed up. So sticking to the plan he had made with his children, Captain Chopra headed to Parliament Street to pick them up. But there was no sign of them. He was informed that Geeta and Sanjay had not come to Akashwani Bhawan that evening. As Captain Chopra rushed home to check if the children had returned, or gone to their friend's home, or had an accident, he did not realize at that time that he would never see them again.

The court documents tell the story through eyewitness accounts and the confessions of the killers themselves. Dr. M.S. Nanda, one of the witnesses, said that while he was driving past the Dhaula Kuan roundabout at about 6.15 pm he saw a young boy and girl asking for a lift towards Connaught Place. Dr. Nanda recalled it was drizzling so he agreed and while the boy sat in the front with him, the girl sat in the rear seat. He related these details several days later to the police who he called after he recognized the Chopra children in a newspaper report about their murder. He told the police that they had chatted with him about doing a radio show and he had dropped them off at the Gole Dak Khana, just a kilometre away from their destination. The last he saw was that they were trying to get another lift to Akashwani Bhawan.

The next witness, Bhagwan Dass told the police he had just left Gurdwara Bangla Sahib at 6.44 pm when he spotted something odd. He saw two men and two children inside a mustard-coloured Fiat standing near the Yoga ashram at Gole Dak Khana. The car's number plate was HRK 8930. Bhagwan Dass heard the words '*Bachao, Bachao!*' (Help, Help) emanating from the car. He then told the police that he abandoned his scooter to run towards the car, especially when he saw that the girl at the back was pulling the hair of the man seated in front of her. The boy was arguing with the man seated next to the driver. Bhagwan Dass says he also saw another person, who had probably seen the same scuffle, try to lunge towards the car door but it was too late, the car sped off.

Passing by Baba Kharak Singh Marg, the Fiat was seen by another witness, Inderjeet Singh, who was also on a scooter and remembered the car overtaking him at Willingdon Hospital (Dr. Ram Manohar Lohia Hospital). At that point, he saw the four occupants inside struggling with each other and the young girl screaming. The boy, realizing he had someone's attention, showed Inderjeet that he was injured and his shoulder was bleeding. Inderjeet started chasing them but at Shankar Road, they jumped the traffic lights and sped away. When Inderjeet went to the police with this report that evening, they failed to inform the control room for at least another hour. A lapse that would cost Geeta and Sanjay Chopra their lives.

Two days later, Dhani Ram, a farm worker, spotted two highly decomposed bodies while out grazing his cattle in the Ridge area.

Captain Chopra soon confirmed that they were the remains of his children, Geeta and Sanjay. According to the post mortem report drawn up by Dr. Bharat Singh on 29 August, three days after they were murdered, Geeta's attractive face was highly decomposed with a blueish hue, and partially destroyed by maggots. Her eyeballs were decomposed and liquefied and her open mouth had left her tongue decomposed too. While her ears were intact, maggots had got to her nose too. The post-mortem noted there were five wounds on her body and while there was no evidence of a violent sexual act, her underwear was missing. Her purse was also found with an identity card, a diary and Rs 17.

In comparison, Sanjay had many cuts across his body – 21 deep incisions to be precise. His head, neck, fingers, thighs, chest had cut marks, as if his killers had momentarily given into a frenzied rage with a sharp object and attacked his entire body. The media carried the discovery of the missing children's bodies with outrage. At the time, Delhi was not the 'rape or murder capital' that it is right now, and it was common for two teenagers to hitch rides, and to make their way around the city by themselves in the evening. As *India Today* reported in its 30 September 1978 issue, Delhi's murder rate then was much lower than the national statistic of one every 20 minutes. In Delhi, there was an attempt to murder once every 30 hours and a murder every 44 hours. A National Crime Records Bureau 2016 report showed Delhi with the highest number of murder cases in the country, with 21.8 per cent followed by Bengaluru with 10.4 per cent and Patna with 8.9 per cent.

Finally shaken out of their inertness, the police were able to zero in on their suspects Jasbir Singh aka Billa aka Bengali and Kuljeet aka Ranga. Both were in their early twenties and had criminal records. In fact, they were in Delhi to evade arrest in Mumbai. On 8 September, exactly two weeks after Geeta and Sanjay were killed, the Kalka Mail train travelling towards Delhi slowed down at a railway crossing just before Agra station. Two civilians got on the train but by chance, they entered the military compartment which was not open to civilians. Lance Naiks Gurtej Singh and AV Shetty immediately objected and asked to see their IDs. Apparently one of the men said to the other, '*Usko bhara hua identity card dikhao*' (show them the ID which is completed). The army jawans immediately suspected their credentials. Lance Naik Shetty happened to have the Hindi newspaper *Navyug* and there it was – a photograph of Billa, the murderer, the same man who had walked into the compartment minutes ago. So at 3.30 am, as the train drew into the Delhi railway station, India's two most wanted men were handed over to the police along with their belongings. Among the items the police recovered was a *kirpan*, a live .32 bore cartridge and bloodstained clothes belonging to both men.

The investigation and trial was able to establish that their blood samples matched those that were found in the Fiat car. The investigation also found that the Chopra children, while resisting their attackers, were able to injure the two enough that they had to seek medical attention. The two men confessed to their crimes in front of a magistrate even though they retracted it later claiming they had only done so under pressure. However, the trial court and the higher courts relied on their confession because it was made after a magistrate took off their handcuffs, asked everyone other than the stenographer to leave the room, and gave them time to rethink their statement. It was this confessional statement which truly revealed the full horror of the crime and the reason the then Prime Minister, Indira Gandhi, was forced to speak about it in Parliament.

As Ranga tells it, the two had run away from Mumbai and came to Delhi ten days before the murder. In need of money, they stole the Fiat car and planned to kidnap a couple and ransack their house. They were going to lure the couple with an offer of a ride and had loosened the door handle of the car so that it would fall if anyone tried to open the door to escape. When they began cruising around Central Delhi for their prey, instead of a couple, they picked up Geeta and Sanjay Chopra because Ranga said they looked like they were from a 'rich family'. Once in the car, the teenagers asked the two where they were taking them. According to Ranga, Billa then began abusing them and asked them to keep quiet, at which point, Geeta pulled his hair while Sanjay kicked Ranga. In retaliation, Ranga took out a small *kirpan* to threaten him but Sanjay tried to snatch it from him and in the process, injured Ranga in the chest. The Chopra children even succeeded in pushing the gear towards neutral and that was why the witness, Bhagwan Dass, had seen the Fiat standing for a while near Gole Dak Khana. But not for long, as it soon sped away to the relatively traffic free Ridge area towards Buddha Garden. Ranga claimed that at various times he suggested they stop the car and release the children but Billa wouldn't listen to him. On reaching Buddha Garden, they were paying for parking when Sanjay asked for water. Ranga said they could have Campa Cola and bought three bottles, but Sanjay refused to drink. Geeta apparently suggested they buy Sanjay him his favourite, an ice-cream.

As Ranga sat with the children in the car, Billa changed the number plates. Ranga then claimed that at this point he got out of the car to tell Billa that their original plan of ransacking the home of the children's parents would not work because he had found out from them that their father was a naval officer. If they tried, the man might shoot them and in any case, it was unlikely they would have that much money in the house.

Ranga also pointed out to the magistrate that he had insisted that the children be set free but Billa did not agree. When Geeta asked why they were waiting in the parking lot of the Buddha Garden, Billa apparently told her they were waiting for a jeweller to arrive from Palam airport at 8.30 pm. He said that if Geeta helped them stop his car to rob him, they would be set free. In reality though, Billa and Ranga were just waiting for darkness to descend. But the car park attendants were restless and so Billa drove towards the airport. The Chopra children again begged to be set free and Ranga said he pleaded their case with Billa yet again. Without heeding any of this, Billa drove back and parked the car on a dirt road near Buddha Garden.

When the two got out the car, Billa asked Ranga to take out the bigger *kirpan* they had bought earlier in the day from Chandni Chowk and hide it at a short distance away. Ranga said he left it about 100 yards away from that area and was walking back when Billa suggested they take Sanjay there. The two led Sanjay away and asked him to lie down. By then Sanjay was pressing a piece of cloth to his wound, and he told the two kidnappers that he had no need to lie down. Billa was getting increasingly impatient and he asked Ranga to get the *kirpan* to finish Sanjay off. As Ranga landed the first blow on his left arm, Sanjay shouted, '*Mat Maro, Mat Maro, Kyon Martey Ho'* (Do not kill, Do not kill! Why are you killing me?). Enraged at Ranga's apparent inefficiency, Billa snatched the *kirpan* and stabbed Sanjay repeatedly for 10 minutes. When he was done, he asked Ranga, 'What are you staring at?' and asked him to hide the body. Ranga later told the judges he did what he was told because he was terrified that if he disobeyed, he would be killed too.

When returned to the car, he witnessed Billa raping Geeta, who was crying for help. Ranga says he went to the road to see if her cries could be heard from afar. He testified that he saw Billa's clothes were lying in the boot of the car, while hers were inside on the dashboard. When he returned around 10-15 minutes later, Billa was done but he told Ranga that he should rape her as well.

Ranga told the magistrate that he protested. In his statement he said, 'I told him that she will give a kick and consequently I shall be flat. Billa again persisted that I should do it. I told him that as I was tall, it was not possible to perform it inside (the car). I suggested to him that in case the seat was taken outside, I would do it. The seat was taken out and was placed by the *dickey*. The girl was perspiring profusely when she was taken out. The girl slipped from the seat as the seat was having slope. At times she was made to lie on the seat. A lot of dust had fallen on her. I kept back. Billa questioned me as to whether I had done my job. I replied him in the affirmative. Billa asked me to let him do the sexual intercourse again. Billa again went for sexual intercourse. At that time I was putting on my clothes.'

Geeta fought her attackers until the end. Ranga in his signed confession says that at this point, Geeta managed to grab the *kirpan* and swung it to hit Billa's forehead. No one made the connection at that point but during trial, this injury that forced Billa and Ranga to stop at the Willingdon Hospital, helped tie up the case. Investigators later found that the doctors had called the police when the duo claimed Billa had been beaten up by someone.

It is fascinating to see how the system at the hospital, in isolation, functioned seamlessly. When Billa (under the fake name 'Vinod') came in to show the wound at 10.15 pm, the doctors alerted the constable on duty at the police post in the hospital. The constable saw the 5½-inch wound that Geeta had managed to inflict and questioned 'Vinod'. His explanation was that someone had snatched his watch by attacking him with an iron rod. When the constable learnt that the attack took place in Mandir Marg, he informed the police station there. But it was only when 'Vinod' left the hospital against medical advice, and when the police found their address and the scooter registration they had given to be fake, that they became suspicious of Billa's story.

Of course at that time, the kidnapping and murder weren't connected with the two men appearing in Willingdon Hospital to get treatment. At the time, no one could link the men to the horrific ordeal that Geeta had to go through before she met her tragic end. According to Ranga's statement after the rape, Geeta ran naked towards the road but he caught her again. Billa told him to just kill her right there, but Ranga said that he had a suggestion.

'I suggested to him to let her wear the clothes. I told the girl that we had made her brother sit with someone and that half an hour time had been given. I questioned the girl saying that in case he sees her naked, what he will say? She wore the *jhagula* (coat) and I helped her in wearing the pants. I suggested to her that I should take her to her brother and that she should go away from there. I was taking her to that side towards which her brother was lying dead. I was on the right hand side of the girl. Billa gave a signal to me and

I got a little ahead. Billa struck the sword with full force against her neck and as a result thereof she was no more alive.' Both the men then picked up her body and threw it into the bush.

These confessions were backed up by circumstantial evidence and that is why the Delhi High Court in their order (before the case went to Supreme Court) termed it the 'cold blooded, ruthless, cruel murders of two young innocent teenagers.' Commenting on the rape and murders, they said Billa and Ranga 'had a fiendish sadistic pleasure in committing the crime,' and so 'to award any other sentence except death sentence will amount to complete failure of justice.' And that is how they ended up in Tihar's *phansi kothi* (hanging room).

~

Decades after I first met Billa and Ranga, I can still distinguish them by their very distinct personalities. Ranga's name in Tihar was 'Ranga *Khush*', a literal representation of his disposition. He was 24-years old and about six-feet tall and eerily, seemed quite happy in jail. '*Ranga Khush, Ranga Khush*' (Ranga's happy). I think he picked this line from the dialogue of a film and used it repeatedly as if to convince himself that he was in a happy place and not on death row. I am not sure whether he was genuinely happy or he had just hypnotized himself into a state, but he kept up his cheery demeanour until the end. In contrast, 22-year-old Billa who was much shorter, only about 5.5 feet tall, would skulk around the jail. Ranga participated in the daily life of the jail community, but Billa did not talk to anyone. He told us repeatedly that he was framed and falsely accused. He would tell his visiting family, 'Get me a lawyer, get me bail.' Every court reaffirmed the death sentence to him but Billa, the man whose blood and his victims' blood had forensically linked him to the crimes, refused to accept it until the end. In contrast, when Ranga's family came to meet him, he would embrace them and that moment with joy and then get on with it. Maybe it is because Ranga truly believed his crime was lesser than Billa's, and that he had tried to free Geeta and Sanjay, but Billa had stopped him. 'They asked us for a lift and we gave it to them. The matter would have finished there. But Billa was attracted to Geeta and that's why it led to such a crime. I only went along.' Of course Billa's version was totally opposite – he claimed that the entire crime was done under the influence of alcohol and that as a family man he was not capable of doing such a thing – Ranga was the rake, the drunken degenerate who indulged and went too far.

This denial of a crime is not common amongst all convicted prisoners, but I have seen it to be true of all rapists. They may cite different reasons for saying why it was not their fault, but they will all claim it was not their doing. In all my work, in all my years in Tihar, I have not seen any convicted rapist admit to his crime. Most blame the victim. They will say that it was not rape at all, it was consensual sex and they were in jail because she wanted to punish him for some reason. Then there are rapists who say that they had consent, that the woman was willing, but they can never explain why she complained to the police. There are also rapists who say that it was a financial arrangement, and that they were victims of circumstances. Yes, there are many variations but they all give themselves a clean chit. Of course, Ranga maintained until the end that when they plotted the kidnapping for ransom, it was never meant to involve rape and murder. It was only when Billa saw Geeta, Ranga claims, that he was overpowered by his attraction towards her and turned a simple kidnap and robbery into the most gruesome rape and murder case that Delhi had ever heard of at the time.

I say all this because a great deal of attention is paid to the psychological status of inmates, especially those on death row. In Tihar, we would generally keep an eye on them and make notes but in other states, jailers were asked to fill extensive psychological study reports. This would ask for notes on habits, temperament, conduct, physical and mental history, whether the inmate came from a broken or a vicious home. A psychologist would also examine them and prepare a report. In Tamil Nadu, this psychological profiling was done for all, but in Maharashtra, it was reserved only for those on death row. For us, the only requirement was that they should not be clinically insane. A clearance on that front made them fit for the noose.

All our psychological profiling on Billa and Ranga led us to one conclusion – they could not stand each other and leaving them together in close proximity was dangerous as they would attack each other physically. As a young jailer, I tried to counsel them against this kind of aggressive behaviour but it is a well-known fact that when a black warrant is issued in your name, you often react with aggression.

The court would issue a black warrant that confirmed the date and time of a convict's hanging. The jailer would seek this when an inmate's mercy petition or multiple petitions were rejected and they had exhausted all means of recourse to challenge the death penalty. We would go to the trial court that had sentenced the convict and ask the judge there to issue this special warrant – titled black warrant because of the black lining all along the edges. Once issued, the prisoner was informed of the time when he would be hanged. In my experience, there are only two ways that people react to this information – either they pick fights, scream, try to hurt you or themselves, and basically resort to violence or they retreat into deep depression, a kind of stunned withdrawal from life. Between Billa and Ranga, we had exhibits of both these reactions.

If the depression takes on a severe degree of mental illness then the rules do not allow the hanging of a prisoner. The logic being the inmate will not be of sound mind to put in review requests, to challenge court orders, etc. It is also against the principle of justice. A mentally ill person is a defenceless person, so by ending such a person's life, are you really bettering society? Prison and punishment serve the purpose of deterrence and hanging a helpless, sick person, goes against everything we stand for. But the stress is, of course, on the word 'degree'. After all, in a way everybody is somewhat mentally ill in jail. Who wouldn't go crazy at the thought of an approaching end? It's only clinically certifiable craziness that can stop a hanging. The insanity plea, for instance, applied in the case of Sundar Singh. Convicted for killing five of his relatives over a land dispute in 2014, Singh got his death sentence commuted to life even though the then President Pranab Mukherjee had rejected his mercy plea. Unlike Billa and Ranga who were certified as sane, the prison doctor who examined Sundar Singh in February 2013 diagnosed him as 'suicidally inclined' and prescribed him strong antipsychotic medicines. Very soon, he was in and out of various institutions like the State Mental Health Institute, Dehradun and Mental Hospital, Varanasi from which he was even released as fit in 2012. But just a year later, he was diagnosed with schizophrenia and the court finally declared him unfit for the death penalty. So, the only escape from hanging is to drive yourself insane.

But it isn't just those who have been served with a black warrant that are battling with reason and sanity. Each of us involved in the process develops various mechanisms to cope with it as we are completely conflicted, some even scared of the consequences of signing such a document. But all of us are mere instruments of the law.

Coming back to the Billa and Ranga case, as soon as the warrant was out and even before the prisoners were placed in their death cells, the summons was sent to Tihar's hangmen – Fakira from Faridkot in Punjab and Kalu from Meerut Jail. These two conducted most of the eight hangings I saw during my time at Tihar. To my knowledge, today there are no professional hangmen left in the country.

I say professional hangmen but in reality hanging was only a part of the responsibilities Fakira and Kalu had as jail officials. Hanging was a well-paying job – for each hanging they got Rs 150 each and a special escort with security to bring them into Tihar and to return them safely to Faridkot and Meerut. They were given a place to stay and their meals were taken care of. The job, however, was a very skillful one and both Kalu and Fakira took great pride in being good at it.

Kalu may have been named so because of his dark skin but Fakira being darker than Kalu was called 'bhoot' (ghost). He had a huge moustache and would always crack jokes in Punjabi, which made all of us laugh. Kalu was quite big built, round and the quieter of the two. They were both extremely professional. As soon as the escort cars brought them in, they would station themselves at the deputy superintendent's ante room, which is like a private room attached to the office.

As you can imagine, a hangman's job comes with strange customs. We have to follow protocol very carefully, as who would want to mess with the gatekeepers of death. One such custom is to give the hangmen a bottle of alcohol each – we would give them Old Monk rum. Consumption of alcohol is strictly forbidden inside the jail premises but as I have mentioned earlier, rules are flouted not just by prisoners but by jailers too. In this particular tradition, it was acceptable to allow the free flow of alcohol before a hanging. I remember Bengal's hangman Nata Mullick's interview where he confessed to drinking heavily before the job. He would stop eating hours before and just drink himself out of any emotion. I don't know if Kalu and Fakira did the same but they seemed very happy when they got their bottle of rum. Nata Mullick also had one other ritual. He would pour some of that booze onto the hanging plank after his work was done. He said it was for the soul of the man he had hanged.

A big fear before the hanging was that the hangman would be kidnapped. I am not sure if there has ever been a case of the hangman gone missing, but it concerned prison officials so much that they did not allow the hangmen to leave the prison complex. The fear was heightened when a terrorist or anyone with a mass following was to be hanged as chances of their supporters doing something desperate was quite possible. 'What if they are taken away by someone?' was the terrifying thought, 'Who will hang the prisoners then?' That's why the movement of the hangmen was kept quite under wraps, even from the jail staff.

There was a reason why Kalu and Fakira worked as a pair. If one hangman developed cold feet, the other would go ahead and finish the job. However, this never happened with our hangmen. They realized they were valuable and so like Nata Mullick, Kalu tried to make it into a family business. They both trained their sons to take over from them. 'I once tried to take an assistant with me,' said Mullick in one of the many interviews that he gave just before he hanged rapist and murderer Dhananjoy Chatterjee on 14 August 2004. Chatterjee had raped and murdered a teenager in 1990. While his punishment was much debated by news channels, it was his hangman who got a considerable amount of media attention. Eighty-three-year old Nata Mullick, exposed people for the very first time to the world of hangings and its mysterious ways. 'As soon as we reached the gallows, he (my assistant) threw up. But my son was fine, I knew that he would be a good apprentice.'

Kalu was so confident that his son would take over that he printed flyers which he sent to our jail and other jails to solicit work. 'Expert hangman. Rent his services.' Of course, we never availed of his services because unlike his father he was not a government employee, which was a prerequisite. We need one of our own to do this work because they were reliable, and bound by law to keep matters confidential. Kalu had obviously calculated that the business of death was lucrative enough for his son to follow his footsteps. According to a Law Commission of India report, between 2000 to 2015, courts gave out death sentences to 1,790 people. Of these 63 per cent were commuted and 29 per cent were acquitted by higher courts. The rest remained pending or their judgements could not be located. Therefore the Law Commission concluded that in roughly 95 per cent of the cases, the death penalty had been wrongly given.

However, there was no doubt about the guilt (or the lack of it) of Billa and Ranga. They were moved to *phansi kothi*, now located in Jail number 3 a week before the black warrant date. This particular part of Tihar has 16 'death cells' as it only houses those in the final week of death row. The hanging area is built within this building, which is completely isolated from other inmates to shield them from seeing the preparations. There are various Supreme Court judgements now that say solitary confinement is a form of torture and should not be inflicted on anyone, but the death cells were considered absolutely necessary. That is why they are under constant surveillance from guards of the Tamil Nadu Special Police (TSP). These guards are stationed for two-hour shifts and are instructed to not take their eyes off the prisoner. It is basically a suicide watch and this is why all their personal belongings are taken away, including items such as pyjama strings which could be used by the prisoner to take his own life. They are not allowed to have any visitors except one final meeting with family and friends. Incidentally, it is up to the prisoner to decide if he even wants this final meeting. Some choose not to. They are also given the opportunity to write a will and the district magistrate is summoned to be a witness to it. In a 24-hour cycle, the inmate is let out to walk around only for a half hour. The rest of the time, he is meant to mentally prepare himself to die.

The news of a black warrant being issued for Billa and Ranga reached the press. I don't know what the source of the leak was, as *Hindustan Times* journalist Prabha Dutt petitioned the superintendent to interview Billa and Ranga. When the prison authorities declined, she went to the top court and soon many other journalists including news agencies followed. In her petition, Prabha Dutt said that it was important to hear their side of the story and in a landmark judgement, the top court agreed, provided the two wanted to meet the journalists. On 30 January 1982, in an unprecedented move, a group of five journalists were led inside Tihar to speak to Billa and Ranga for the last time. However, Ranga did not agree to speak to either Prabha Dutt or the others. In those limited minutes that the reporters were allowed to interact with Billa, he pledged his innocence one last time.

On the night before they were hanged, I was on duty outside the death cell along with three other officers. We were to ensure that the guards posted to watch the two were doing their job. So, we sat in the superintendent's room and waited. It is hard to find the right words to describe my mood that day. I could not eat dinner that night because of what was to come and the adrenaline I was experiencing made me feel a little guilty. Every hour or so, I would walk to their cell to observe what they were doing. Unlike me, Ranga calmly ate his dinner and was able to turn in for the night and to sleep just like it was any other night, and not his last. On the other hand, Billa neither ate nor slept. He was just pacing inside his cell, muttering to himself and telling anyone who cared to listen that he was innocent and that Ranga was the one who was to blame. But his claims would fall on deaf ears – their mercy petitions had been exhausted and even though there had been a few instances in Tihar's history when hangings were stopped at the eleventh hour, no one expected any last minute interventions in this case. In one such case, a hanging was stalled when a woman inmate was given a last medical test and they discovered she was pregnant. But however heinous the crimes of people are, you develop a relationship with them, and are still moved when you see them cry because they are afraid of death. Ranga saw Billa's tears and mocked him '*Dekho mard hoke ro raha hai!*' (Look at this pathetic man who cries!).

The next morning on the last day of January 1982, Tihar was ready for D-Day. The entire Jail Road was shut down. The media was standing outside hoping to get something, anything. Of course, they were not going to be able to see anything, not even a glimpse of visiting family members. Because the *phansi kothi* is the most obscure area and well hidden from public view. There is not much to distinguish this hanging room except for the hanging platform with a well that is 15 feet deep. The well was covered by two wooden boards that were held together by an iron rod. Above this well is the metal bar from which hangs the noose. There is a lever on the side and when that is pulled, the wooden boards part plunging the person standing on the boards to be suspended suddenly. Theoretically, this should lead to instant death but as we soon found out, it varies.

Billa and Ranga were given a cup of tea each when they woke up in the morning. It seems the best of prison services is made available to inmates when they are about to die because for once all their rights are adhered to strictly. They were asked for the last time if they wanted a magistrate to note their will. Both Billa and Ranga declined. The prisoners are then encouraged to shower and are dressed in black. Their hands and legs are handcuffed and just 10 minutes before the time stated on the black warrant they are brought to the execution platform. As far as the rules go, Maharashtra is one state which allows the families of the prisoner to witness their hanging if they wish to. But Delhi state rules do not have any such provision and only jail officials were present.

And so early that morning of 31 January 1982, we watched as the noose was put around Ranga and Billa's neck and their faces were covered so that they could not see what was happening around them. Billa was sobbing and crying but Ranga was triumphant until the end shouting, '*Jo Bole So Nihaal, Sat Stri Akal*!' At the moment they plunged to their death, I noticed the colour of their face change. It is as if the skin changes colour and turns black out of fear, a fear that is transparent in their eyes. And before we knew what happened, Kalu, assisted by Fakira pulled the lever and Billa and Ranga collapsed into the well.

Our jail manuals tell us that death in these cases is instantaneous. The sudden collapse of the plank and the suspension into the air causes the vertebrae to break leading to death. This is the ideal situation, which is what hangmen aim for. But in my very first hanging, something very strange happened. As per protocol, when the doctor checked the two, after two hours, it appeared that while Billa had died, Ranga still had a pulse. We were told that since he was slim and tall and had held his breath, he had managed to survive the hanging. So one jail staff was given the task to jump into the well beneath his hanging body and pull his legs. The guard did as he was told and in this fashion, the last breath of Ranga's life was finally pulled out of him. Fortunately, it was not until thirty-two years later that the Shatrughan Chauhan judgement was issued, stating that a post-mortem was mandatory for any prison hanging. Else word would have got out that Ranga's hanging needed 'external help'.

But no one found out or cared too much at the time. Neither Billa nor Ranga's family came to claim their bodies and it was left to us to cremate them both. The superintendent of prisons signed the undertaking stating that he had carried out the executions. As I went home, I noticed Prabha Dutt was waiting outside Tihar unaware of the last-minute drama that had transpired with the two. Her story and that of four other journalists was front page news – with Billa proclaiming how he was framed due to Ranga's exploits.

As per the provision of jail manual, the superintendent of jail is required to direct the hangman to pull the lever of the wooden plank on which the prisoner to be hanged is standing. The superintendent at that time, A.B. Shukla, had waved a red-coloured handkerchief to signal the hangman to pull the lever. He used to show this red handkerchief to his friends, who were amazed to see the same handkerchief that was used to signal the hanging of Ranga and Billa.

I went home and went about my day normally. I realized that witnessing a hanging had not impacted me that much. Did I talk about it with my family? Not really. I did not have the words.

THE ANATOMY OF A HANGING

The day before an execution prisoner goes through a harrowing experience of being weighed, measured for length of drop to assure breaking of the neck, the size of the neck, body measurements etc. When the trap springs he dangles at the end of rope. There are times when the neck has not been broken and the prisoner strangles to death. His eyes pop almost out of his head, his tongue swells and protrudes from his mouth, his neck may be broken and the rope many times takes large portion of skins and flesh from the side of the face that the noose is on. He urinates, he defecates and droppings fall to the floor while witnesses look on and at almost all executions one or more faint or have to be helped out of the witness room. The prisoner remains dangling from the end of the rope from 8 to 14 minutes before the Doctor, who has climbed up a small ladder and listen to his heartbeat with a stethoscope, pronounces him dead. A prison guard stands at the feet of the hanged person and holds the body steady, because during the first few minutes there is usually considerable struggling in an effort to breathe.

– Warden Duffy of San Quention Prison
Law Commission of India, 187th Report

This is the horrific reality which I may have played down when I told you the story of Billa and Ranga's hanging. We did not focus on these details as we watched it unfold in front of our eyes. At that time, the idea of a constable jumping into the well to pull the prisoner's legs so that his pulse would stop was not as reprehensible to us as it may be to you. We were told that it happens sometimes. Especially when an inmate who is really, really terrified of what was going to happen to him, stops breathing. Like everything else in life, horror is relative. For instance, if the rope measurement was wrong and the drop of the body was too long, then the head would have been torn off the body. Legend has it, that this 'accident' has happened before. The story has been passed on to us like the collective nightmare that refuses to be erased. Maybe, that is why they stopped allowing families of the prisoners to be present at the hanging.

On the subject of relatives, a 1970s manual from Maharashtra prisons says that adult male relatives of the inmate and other 'respectable male adults' – not more than 12 in number – may be allowed to watch the hanging (female relatives have never been allowed to be present). But can you just imagine what would happen if families did witness the hanging? What if they saw their loved one's head being yanked off? The actual act is gruesome enough without having to put them through this.

There are detailed instructions about who can be present at the hanging. Apart from the doctor who issues the certificate declaring the prisoner dead, there are 10 constables, two head constables or an equal number of the prison's armed guards. This manual also mentions the need to have a *jamadar* or sweeper because as you can imagine from the description above, the remains of a hanging can be extremely messy. This is why I think we have to dress the prisoner in black so that when his bowels and bladder empty, it is not too visible. It is also the reason why I will always associate death with the stench of a toilet. Today hangings are always indoors (behind enclosures within the jails) but in the past there was a provision to make examples of the prisoners, and thus other prisoners were made to watch the execution. This was done to serve as a deterrent. Suppose the execution was of someone who was in prison for a lesser crime but was later sentenced to death because they killed another inmate. In such a case, the superintendent could decide to allow other prisoners to watch the execution – to send a message to them. However, in most cases today, prisoners are not allowed to witness the hanging because it can lead to rioting amongst them. But then how do you make an example of hanging without doing ISIS-style public executions and then circulating pictures of it? The rules state that all the prison authorities need to do is to inform the district magistrate of the area where the sentenced person is from. Using the old fashioned method of beating drums, they would inform the entire village or town that the person having committed murder was being hanged in so and so jail and 'let all evil minded persons take note, (Govt Resolution, Judicial Department number 6049, dated September 7, 1898). Fortunately, innovations in mass media and being in a big, urban city like Delhi, ensured that we never had to publicize our executions in such a manner.

Hanging someone is a complicated business practically as well. We did what was in our control to ensure that the hanging went as smoothly as possible for everyone involved – especially the prisoner. Along with the hangmen, we practised the routine a number of times with bags of sand weighing 1.5 times the weight of the prisoner. While we did not need to buy a new rope for every hanging, we did have to carefully use wax or butter to smoothen it. Some hangmen had their own unique methods of preparing the rope, such as carefully treating it with mashed bananas. The rope would then be securely locked away by the deputy superintendent of the jail until the date of the hanging. The length of the rope is just enough to allow the drop of either 1.8 or 2.4 metres, depending on the weight of the person to be hanged. So, say if the prisoner weighed under 45 kilos, then the longest drop of 2.4 metres was required, but if he was heavier, then it was a much shorter drop of 6 feet or 1.8 metres for anyone above 90 kilos.

This was not the only calculation we had to do. We had to take the height of the prisoner from the floor to his jaw immediately below his left ear, the height of the beam to which the rope is fixed and the neck measurements – these details are noted diligently to make arrangements for the hangman. The length of rope is the length of the drop, plus the distance from the angle of the prisoner's jaw, to the ring. That was all fine in theory but in practice, the hangman would pride himself on calculating everything by guesswork. He would just need to look at the sentenced man to decipher how many bags of sand were needed to test the ropes. Finally, one last calculation was done for the hanging, that of measuring the neck. The heavier the person, the longer their neck would elongate during the process. This would give an indication of whether the person would actually die of dislocation of the cervical vertebrate, which is the quickest and most painless way to die. After all, the law and our Constitution demands that the system be just and fair – even for a condemned man.

This is the reason why in 2014, the Supreme Court made it mandatory through the Shatrughan Chauhan judgement to conduct post-mortems even after capital punishment. This ended the, at times, arbitrary way in which hangmen or prison officials operated, for whom executions were simply the quickest way of ending a life. For some, hanging the condemned man quickly was their sole objective and so they did not pay attention to the intricate details that were laid out in the official manuals. This was unfortunate because these rules try to induce some dignity into the hanging process. For instance, the rule which says that you have to deal with mercy petitions swiftly otherwise it is torture for the prisoner, has been time and again flouted by prison officials. There are so many instances of this happening, like in the case of Sonia and Sanjiv Kumar from Haryana.

To say that the two committed a brutal crime in August 2001 would be an understatement. The duo used an iron rod to club to death Sonia's father, Relu Ram, an MLA from Haryana and seven other family members over a property dispute. Sonia and Sanjiv's victims included two children, aged two and three months. When the gruesome details of how the couple killed their own family members emerged in the media, it shocked the entire country and resulted in the judge's deciding on the death penalty for the two of them. The defence's plea that Sonia tried to commit suicide after committing the crime was not enough to save her. But it was truly death by torture. The state did not only sentence the couple to death, they kept their mercy petition hanging for six-and-a-half years. They spent this time on death row, in solitary confinement because those who are sentenced to death are isolated from the rest of the prison population. So a petition which is supposed to be decided in 15 days and used to be dealt with quite swiftly in the 1980s took more than five years to be decided upon by the president. After this delay, the honourable judges decided that so many years of 'mental agony' was a good enough punishment and commuted their death sentence.

Much before, in 1974, Justice Krishna Iyer had touched upon the 'brooding horror haunting the prisoner in the condemned cell for years'. The top court of the country had been sensitized to this pain so long ago, and yet from the 15 days to decide on mercy petitions, the delays slowly stretched to 11 months and then four years by 1988 and by the time this landmark Shatrughan Chauhan judgement was given in 2014, some people had been on death row for more than 12 years.

Can you even imagine what it is like to spend 12 years without any human interaction? To have just 30 minutes in a day to stretch your legs and rest of the time to just stare at the walls without even having a pencil, pen, not even your pyjama's drawstrings because the state fears you could use any of these to end your miserable existence? It is not because our laws enable such cruelty. On the contrary, there are many judgements and even the 1860 Indian Penal Code says that solitary confinement is a form of torture. But in the garb of prisoner safety, the Prison Act Section 30 says you should keep such people 'apart from other prisoners', in other words, solitary confinement.

This pain, this excruciating agony of impending death is called 'death row phenomenon'. One Supreme Court judge even uses an Albert Camus reference from 'Reflections on the Guillotine', an essay written in 1957 to describe it:

> ...For the man condemned to death, on the other hand, the horror of his situation is served up to him at every moment for months on end. Torture by hope alternates only with the pangs of animal despair. His lawyer and his confessor, out of simple humanity, and his guards, to keep him docile, unanimously assure him that he will be reprieved. He believes them with all his heart, yet he cannot believe them at all. He hopes by day, despairs by night. And as the weeks pass his hope and despair increase proportionately, until they become equally insupportable. According to all accounts, the color of his skin changes: fear acts like an acid. "It's nothing to know if you're going to die," one such man in the Fresnes prison said, "but not to know if you're going to live is the real torture." ...As a general rule, the man is destroyed by waiting for his execution long before he is actually killed. Two deaths are imposed, and the first one is worse than the second, though the culprit has killed but once.

On paper we have rules that bind the government and the prison officials to ensure that no one is put through this torture before they are hanged. Every jail manual and judgement, informs the jail superintendent that they must give the inmate at least a week to file their mercy petition, and this must be in an express manner so that the president or the governor, whoever receives it, knows that it has to be decided upon urgently. And until the president decides whether his mercy is worth bestowing, they should not be put on death row or in solitary confinement.

But of course the reality is different – model rules to tackle cruelty like the 'death row phenomenon' which was drafted in

2003, have still not been implemented. The reality is that we, the prison staff, should be using a red envelope with the words 'Death Sentence' and 'Immediate' for all such communication so that it is dealt with quickly. But there have been times when we have hanged prisoners without giving them the required week's notice to prepare themselves for their end.

The story of Surendra Koli illustrates how monumentally wrong we are at times. Perhaps Koli's rights were disregarded because he was sentenced to death for one of the most heinous crimes the country has seen. He and his employer Moninder Singh Pandher were held guilty for the rape and murder of a 14-year-old girl called Rimpa Haldar. While the conviction was only for this one victim, the remains of at least 16 others (mostly children) were found on the grounds of their home. Police believed that they had been killed between 2005 and 2006. The well-off businessman Pandher was later acquitted by the high court but Koli, the poor housekeeper, had no one to defend him. The media had gone to town about stories of cannibalism which were never proved but were ingrained in the minds of the people and, perhaps, the jail officials as well.

According to legal documents, the state did not bother to inform Koli that the then President Pranab Mukherjee had rejected his mercy petition in July 2014. It was only when he was moved two months later to Meerut Jail from Dasna, where he had spent his entire jail sentence since 2006, that Koli realized something was wrong. He was told he was being shifted because there were no hanging facilities in Dasna Jail. In spite of not informing him, the administration managed to get a black warrant for him. Koli was able to send word to his lawyers who moved court at 1 am on 8 September, as the next day he was to be hanged. The court, however, gave the team a week's time, and Koli went back to Dasna awaiting further word on his fate.

It is a small consolation but by then he had become quite used to waiting as he had been in solitary confinement since 2009, when he was sentenced to death by the trial court. They did not even want the higher courts to confirm it, and simply isolated him while his appeal for mercy stacked up a record number of delays. The Uttar Pradesh government took two-and-a-half years to move his file, the central government took seven-and-a-half months and when this file movement of two-and-a-half years ended in a rejection, they did not bother informing Koli that his time was up. They simply moved him from his solitary cell in Dasna to one in Meerut jail, right next to the *phansi kothi*. Surendra Koli was probably at the edge of his sanity when eventually, he had some good news. In January 2015, the Allahabad High Court said that the delay of three years and three months in deciding Koli's mercy petition was unconstitutional and against his right to life and his death sentence was commuted to life.

Koli can thank the court and fate for intervening and saving his life. But others have not been so lucky, the most notable of them being Maqbool Butt, a Kashmiri separatist who faced trial in a Delhi court. When an Indian diplomat was murdered in the name of free Kashmir, a collective conscience needed to be sated and I was witness to how Butt was hanged almost overnight for something that he was only remotely linked to.

~

Jis dhaj se koi maqtal mein gaya wo shaan salamat rehti hai,
Ye jaan to aani jaani hai, is jaan ki to koi baat nahin.
(The glory that one carries to the gallows survives;
this life is transitory, it's not of great importance)
– Faiz Ahmed Faiz as quoted by Maqbool Butt

I will remember Maqbool Butt, not as the founder of the Jammu and Kashmir Liberation Front (JKLF), a separatist group from the Valley, but as the highly educated, pious inmate with whom I used to practice my English language skills. The 45-year-old separatist leader was from a village in Kupwara where he did his early education before crossing over to Pakistan where he pursued his degree in literature at Peshawar University. He was passionate about the freedom of Kashmir. He had crossed over to Pakistan in the 1950s when there was a crackdown on Sheikh Abdullah's supporters in Kashmir. He settled in Pakistan and worked as a journalist but it was politics and the fight for an independent Kashmir which again brought him back to India in 1966. When I met him in Tihar, he was serving out a death sentence for killing a CID officer while trying to cross over to Pakistan. The murder meant being sentenced to death but he didn't stay in the Srinagar jail for too long. Just two years later, he and another inmate dug a 38-foot tunnel to escape to Muzaffarabad in Pakistan Occupied Kashmir (PoK). Butt's dramatic escape did not last long and he was arrested in PoK, too. When he was freed three months later, he went on to commit the act that branded him an anti-national for life – the hijacking and blowing up of an Indian Airlines flight to Lahore in 1971. All the passengers were returned safely but this didn't go down well with Pakistan authorities, who had to face consequences like India banning all over flights to Bangladesh. Such actions increased the already heightened tensions between the nations that eventually culminated in the 1971 war. Maqbool found himself in jail again, this time in Pakistan, and was there for three years along with the fellow hijackers Hashim and Ashraf Qureshi. After his release, he tried his hand at Pakistani politics but when that did not work out, he headed back to India in 1980, where he was soon captured and the decade-old death sentence was reiterated by the Supreme Court. This time there was no escape for him because he was moved to Tihar. And that's where I met him in the high-security ward.

It was very clear that Maqbool was a political prisoner and he was treated as one too. Unlike others who would spend their time gossiping or trying to make trouble, all he did was read. When he took a break from reading, he would regale us with his discourse on Kashmir and why he was fighting for its freedom from India and Pakistan. Or he would tell us stories of his travels between India and Pakistan and the various adventures he undertook. It was fascinating and we were a bit in awe of this international figure, even though he was considered anti-India. We could see why he had a massive following in Kashmir and abroad. Maqbool was a preacher of Islam and its philosophy and I noticed how he was equally dismissive of PoK, as he was of India. He was fighting for the good for his community and for his beliefs. Anyway, we did not pay much attention to his principles because we were too busy making his erudition useful for us. We would head to his ward to help us with memos, chargesheets, any kind of documentation. I was still a fresher and was happy with the assistance. Butt was simple and well-mannered, really a first-class man. It was because of this attitude and his studious nature that he was one of those rare prisoners on death row who was not put in a solitary cell. Initially, when he first came from Srinagar, we had put him in a solitary cell but he made a very convincing argument against it in the high court by calling out the prison officials' bluff. He threw the rule book at them against such a lockup and the high court agreed. As in everything else in prison, these diktats are based on flimsy grounds and are usually the whims of the jailer, so educated prisoners like Butt or those who can hire a proper lawyer, do not find it too difficult to reason it out.

To say that he was a religious man who did his namaz five times a day would be an understatement. The Quran was his constant companion and he would do regular readings, taking on the halo of being a man of God for the people in Tihar, rather than a terrorist. There was nothing he loved more than inmates or guards reaching out to him with queries. And when he was not busy with his intellectual pursuits, he would play volleyball with other inmates.

Certain prisoners leave a legacy of long-term reform and I am not talking about the plugging of security loopholes which were carried out after Sobhraj's escape. I am referring to doing good; about actually opening society's eyes to the potential of improving the lives of inmates. For instance, the world knows IPS officer R.K. Sharma as the man who faced trial for conspiring to murder journalist Shivani Bhatnagar in 1998. Tihar inmates, however, know him as the man who fought for the rights of inmates to make phone calls from Tihar. It led to phonecards and an allotted few minutes a day on previously verified phone numbers of family members. This was a simple but significant step that prisoners thanked Sharma for long after he left jail. Similarly, Butt contributed to changes in the inmates' lives in two ways. First, he petitioned authorities about stocking religious books in jail. His argument was if jail was a correctional facility then for a lot of people that route was via spirituality. How can prisoners be influenced by spirituality if they do not have access to religious texts such as the Quran, the Gita or the Bible? It was hard to dispute this and so we agreed.

The other impact that Butt made was more dramatic. When he reached Tihar, we were still bound by the British prison manual which said stationery was contraband in jail. Apparently, there was a fear that prisoners may write and smuggle out incendiary material so writing instruments and material was kept away from inmates. This became another battle that Butt fought and won for other prisoners and won. I cannot remember a single instance when he created a problem for us or broke any rules. If he fought the system, it was by petitioning authorities in the right manner. Even his jail uniform (white kurta pyjama) was always pristine, spotless and sparkling. Just like his prison record.

To my mind, Butt was a victim of circumstances. I always felt that if the Indian diplomat, Ravindra Mhatre, had not been kidnapped and murdered in Birmingham, Butt would have stayed in jail for a long time, despite serving out a death sentence. It was rumoured that Butt could be released as a good-will gesture to speed up the process of integration. But his fate was sealed as soon as news came in on 3 February 1984 that the assistant high commissioner at the Indian consulate in Birmingham had been kidnapped and an unknown group, Kashmir Liberation Front (KLF), had claimed responsibility. They had also demanded the release of Maqbool Butt.

There were no known links between Butt's JKLF and the KLF apart from their pro-separatist views. But as India woke up to the news of Mhatre's killing, within 24 hours of his kidnapping, there was a collective anger to which Indira Gandhi's government had to respond. This was the first and only case of an Indian diplomat being targeted by a militant Kashmiri group. There were news reports speculating whether India had taken too long to respond, whether the crisis management group could have responded quicker to avert the killing and buy time, etc. And so, the government believed that quick, retributive action needed to be taken that would send out a message that India was not a pushover.

On 6 February 1984, just hours after the Indian government was informed about the discovery of Mhatre's body with three bullets pumped into it, the cabinet committee on political affairs led by Prime Minister Indira Gandhi decided to hang Butt immediately. I believe they wanted to tell the world and the militants that 'if you kill one of our officers, we'll kill one of yours'. While Mrs. Gandhi got in touch with the then J&K chief minister, Farooq Abdullah, who would have to deal with local repercussions, they moved files to reject Butt's pending mercy petition. While all of this unfolded on the radio which he had access to, Butt took it all in with a stoicism that we found difficult to understand. Though nothing was conveyed to him directly, he seemed to know that it was going to impact him directly. Things were happening very quickly. The Director General of Prisons R.S. Sethi immediately took off for Srinagar, ostensibly to get Butt's black warrant. Usually, this was left to people like me but this time, they wanted the top legal officer to ensure nothing went wrong and to expedite the paperwork.

As we began preparations for the hanging, Butt's lawyers also moved fast. They went to the Supreme Court questioning the propriety of what they saw as 'retributive action'. Calling it a 'judicial murder', they claimed that the high court judgement was unsigned. I remember this lawyer very well. Also a Kashmiri, R.M. Tufail used to come to Tihar with Butt's brother, Ghulam Nabi. Like his brother, Ghulam was very well-mannered but Tufail was aggressive. He knew that the high court needed to sanction the exact time of the execution and he claimed that the proper procedure had not been followed because the judge had not put his initials on this document of the court. This became an object of contention in the Supreme Court with just a handful of days left for Butt's hanging slated on 12 February 1984. Kapil Sibal and Muzaffar Beg, both now politicians and senior advocates, fought for the rights of Maqbool Butt. But the Supreme Court bench hearing the matter told them there was nothing wrong at all with the black warrant, it was perfectly kosher. And so almost instantly, Butt's legal recourses were disposed off. This was the 1980s when we did not even have STD phones, forget about all the fast modes of communication we have now. There was only telex and telephones and yet, because the state wanted it to be so, mercy petitions, review petitions were all dealt within only three to four days.

It is fair to say that I had mixed feelings about Butt's hanging. I enjoyed our interactions, he was wise, and we had all learnt many new things from him. I was also three years into my job and by now had some worldliness as a prison officer. I realized that you could be friends with someone while knowing the inevitability of their situation. At the same time, Butt was being punished for his anti-India ideology and so, despite all that we shared, I knew that this was the right thing to happen to him.

To be honest, I was a bit excited. This was not some loathsome criminal being hanged like Billa or Ranga. Butt was a political prisoner and so the top authorities of the country were tracking this execution very carefully as there was a lot at stake for everyone. Plus there was the added pressure of the possible repercussions. Intelligence reports came in to warn us that Butt's supporters from across the world could do anything – they could plan an attack on the jail itself in order to rescue him. Can you imagine what that was like for a young prison officer? Would there be an air strike or would they just raid the prison? The Intelligence Bureau (IB) left nothing to chance. They shut down all roads that led to Tihar and increased surveillance around it. Section 144 of the Criminal Procedure Code, which bars the gathering of four people or more, was imposed and no one could gain access to Tihar.

It was also because of this security concern that Ghulam wanted to rush to see his brother, but he was not allowed. According to newspaper reports, despite all that is written in the jail manuals about allowing prisoners to have one last meeting with their families, Ghulam was arrested at Srinagar airport. Tufail came to see his client for one last time, but was also denied a meeting.

While all requirements were done away with for this extraordinary case, what we did grant him, according to rules, was the opportunity to leave a will. I remember that a Sikh magistrate was called in a day before the hanging, who asked him if he wanted to write a will. Butt said that he did not have a will but he did have a message he wanted to be conveyed. He got his will recorded by the sub-divisional magistrate in English, in which he exerted, 'There will be many Maqbool Butts that will come and go, but the freedom struggle in Kashmir should continue'. Butt did not know this at the time but his friends, family and the people of Kashmir would never read this message. We realized the sensitivity and the potential inflammatory consequences that such a message would have and so we sent it to the office of the concerned government authority, and never heard about it again.

As Butt read his namaz for the last time, drank tea, and went quietly to the gallows, he was the picture of serenity. His legal team had tried until the very last minute to stall the execution. They called it a 'judicial murder' and gave statements to the media, but the public anger over Mhatre's murder exceeded the need to follow rules in Butt's case. Apparently, when Tufail last spoke to Butt, he had this exchange which he later shared with us, 'I believe you are quite a trained person in various activities. Have you ever thought of escaping?' Butt apparently told him, 'There's no place to escape to. Because I don't find the pride of Kashmiris in India or in Pakistan.'

Early morning on 11 February, a sub-divisional magistrate oversaw the hanging of Maqbool Butt. There were no outsiders present and it was decided that because Butt's hanging was going to lead to a volatile situation, he would be buried in Tihar itself. The government felt that if his body was handed over to his family, separatist supporters would make a martyr of him, and the movement for Kashmiri freedom would spiral out of control. This posed a major challenge for us because no one had been buried inside Tihar before.

In Tihar, like in many other jails in India, the Muslim population of inmates is about 25 per cent. A small number of this comprises Kashmiri prisoners and as anticipated, on the day of Butt's hanging, some of them protested. I don't remember it being a very significant protest but some prisoners did not eat their meals. Never once, however, did we fear that there was going to be a rebellion. And that was because of the way jail authorities have a built in system of submission. Every prisoner is kept in check by a head prisoner, who is then kept in check by a ***numberdar***. They are all doing time and yet they all revel in their authority over the other, negating any possibility of them uniting to rebel against the authorities. If any inmate creates trouble, they risk a brutal backlash from the others and so in jail it is every man for himself, unless a common facility risks being taken away. Each one is too busy extracting favours from the jail staff to unite on religious or caste lines. This was why when we asked Muslim inmates to prepare Butt's grave, we did not hear any murmurs of displeasure. They did what was asked of them: they dug his last resting place, cleaned his body before putting it in Tihar's first grave and poured back the soil on his body. Also, a Muslim clergy from a nearby masjid was present to carry out the rituals.

The day after the hanging, Tufail and other members of his legal team tried to come to Tihar to retrieve Butt's belongings, to give to his family in Srinagar. However, they were detained two kilometres away from the jail. Butt's family also met me several times to take his belongings but there was nothing I could do for them. Just as the state decided Butt's last letter should stay hidden, so would his books and his kurta pyjama. So for a long time, I think these were just left lying around somewhere in Tihar. I do not know what became of his other belongings, but at some point his books (which included works of Sartre and Will Durant) became a part of the library in Jail number 3. In the years to come, those who borrowed these books had no idea who they once belonged to. As for his family, I had little idea what happened to them though I later learnt that his brother Ghulam Nabi was killed in Kashmir.

The absurdity and tragedy of the way Butt was hanged can be seen by the following incident. Justice Anand's court had scheduled a hearing of Maqbool Butt's case a few days later where they were officially informed that the 45-year-old petitioner had been hanged, just a week before his birthday. The Delhi High Court judge sent a notice to the government asking why had he been hanged when his case was still under review in court. We informed the honourable judge that the orders to hang him came directly from the competent authority. And there ended the judicial fight against Maqbool Butt's hanging.

~

The *phansi kothi* was never the most pleasant part of Tihar jail. Even when I joined, I remember people avoided it unless a prisoner had to be punished. If anyone misbehaved or broke the rules, they would be kept there as a punishment. The entire area was said to be haunted and some people even heard sounds at night. These stories became more exaggerated after Butt's hanging.

I admit to becoming wary about the *phansi kothi* only after Butt's hanging and would ask a helper or a guard to accompany me. I purposely avoided looking towards his grave. I remember once walking by and an inmate shouted out, 'Sir, Sir! See Maqbool is standing there.' He was crying and swore that he saw him standing wearing his signature white kurta pyjama.

Inmates housed near the *phansi kothi* were the ones we categorized as the most dangerous. But even the most hardened prisoners refused to stay there alone and we decided to club three of them together in a cell. One morning, we found an inmate murdered in his cell close to the *phansi kothi*. If this was not disturbing enough, when questioned, the one who had done the deed claimed that he had been possessed by the spirit of Maqbool Butt. Of course, this was a very weak excuse and he failed to convince anybody. No one in Tihar could believe that even the ghost of Maqbool Butt was capable of harming anybody.

However, it must be said here that these stories were not limited to just prisoners. The Tamil Nadu Special police guarding the area also reported similar stories. Many of them apparently 'saw' Maqbool Butt standing near his grave. Some even said that he came and grabbed them by the neck. Every time someone raised an alarm like this, extra forces would rush to the ward, but they would find nothing there. Ghost stories relating to Maqbool Butt live on even today in Tihar.

They are not all scary though. Some inmates truly believe in the benevolent spirit of Maqbool Butt. They have told me how he came to them in their dream and told them they would be free soon. And in some cases, apparently proved to be true.

THE MEN WHO KILLED INDIRA GANDHI

Billa and Ranga in 1982, Maqbool Butt in 1984, Kartar and Ujagar Singh in 1985, Satwant and Kehar Singh in 1989, and finally, Afzal Guru in 2013. This is the roll call of the hanged men that provide the most morbid highlights of my career, ensuring that they and I will always be inextricably linked. If I reflect upon these cases one by one, I can see evolving trends or patterns that are very recognizable in our society today. The sadistic duo of Billa and Ranga forever robbed Delhi of the innocent belief that young women and children could move freely without fear on its streets. Butt, the separatist anti-national, terrified the State so much that they removed all traces of him, even his last words. In the case of Kartar and Ujagar Singh, it showed how our justice system favoured the rich and powerful. All of these cases became leitmotifs for crime and punishment in India.

Justice Kochchar was a visibly distressed man when he signed the black warrants for the two brothers – Kartar and Ujagar Singh. I was the one who had to collect the warrant from him and it was apparent that he had misgivings. The two men were very poor, so poor that they could not even afford decent counsel. The two had been hired by Dr. Narendra Singh Jain (who was the personal eye surgeon to the then president, Dr. V.V. Giri) for only Rs 500 to murder his wife, Vidya. The murder was planned by Dr. Jain and his co-conspirator Chandresh Sharma, who was his secretary as well as lover. The two had worked together but their affair had been discovered by Vidya who had then got Chandresh fired. Dr. Jain with his paramour then made an elaborate plan to get rid of Vidya.

On 4 December 1973 as Dr. Jain and Vidya were leaving their home in posh Defence Colony in south Delhi, Chandresh, who was waiting nearby, signalled to the two hitmen to attack Vidya. While Kartar pinned her down, Ujagar used a knife to stab her 14 times, killing her almost instantly. The entire plot was soon unravelled by the prosecution because there were so many holes in the case. There was no apparent motive for the attack on Vidya. Why did Dr. Jain not raise an alarm when the killers attacked his wife? Why was he spared? The details of this case shocked us all but what was particularly strange is that the trial court's life sentence for all the accused was amended by the high court, which gave the death sentence only to the hitmen and spared Chandresh and Dr. Jain, who were sentenced to life imprisonment instead.

It was apparent that Kartar and Ujagar, who spent their time peacefully in jail, doing mundane work such as carpentry, knew why they had met their fate while the others had got away. In their late fifties, they told me, 'If we had a good lawyer representing us, this wouldn't have happened.' The Delhi High Court ruled that the crime of the conspirators, Jain and Chandresh's was 'at a lower plane' than the hitmen and enhanced their punishment 'to be hanged by the neck till they are dead'. So Kartar and Ujagar were hanged to death on 9 October 1983 while the two lovers who had planned it all, were spared. In fact, two years after the hanging, on 22 July 1985, the Delhi High Court accepted Dr. Jain and his lover's application that they had been punished enough by spending 16 years in jail. While Dr. Jain had exemplary conduct on his side, Chandresh had attacked a woman matron in jail so the same could not be said about her. Nevertheless, their lawyers were able to get them off and they were set free.

Not all plotters have it so easy though. The next men to be hung in Tihar were the killer and the 'plotter' of a brutal political assassination. Another man was almost hanged at the same time. His crime? He was a Sikh police officer who took a lot of days off work, arousing suspicion. Fortunately for him, high-profile lawyers like Ram Jethmalani and P.N. Lekhi took an interest in his case.

~

On 31 October 1984, Prime Minister Indira Gandhi left her home on Safdarjung Road in the Capital to walk a few steps to her home-cum-office in an attached bungalow on Akbar Road. An Irish television crew along with the actor and writer Peter Ustinov was waiting to interview her. It would have been a very newsy interview because in the summer gone by, Mrs. Gandhi had conducted a controversial operation to eliminate Sikh militants led by a radical sect leader Jarnail Singh Bhindranwale, who was rallying for a separate state of Khalistan. Codenamed Operation Bluestar, the mission which was to flush out armed militants from inside the Golden Temple was very controversial because it meant that the army had to enter the Sikhs' holiest shrine to flush out militants who were hiding inside there. It was Prime Minister Indira Gandhi who had ordered the army to go in. During the operation, Bhindranwale and his militants were either killed or captured but the gunfire and ammunition caused tremendous damage to the Harmandir Sahib. More than the physical impact, Sikhs across the world were enraged that their holy shrine had been desecrated and turned into a battle zone in which hundreds were killed. Though one can argue that the operation may have been a strategic necessity, it led to deep resentment within the Sikh community against the prime minister. And that, according to the prosecution, compelled a few Delhi Police personnel who were her Sikh bodyguards, to plan and carry out the attack against Indira Gandhi.

The case files say that Constable Satwant Singh and Sub-Inspector Beant Singh were on the prime minister's protection duty on 31 October. Sub-inspector Balbir Singh was also rostered but came on his shift much later at 3 pm. Apparently, Beant and Satwant Singh had swapped their shifts with others so that they would be exactly at the spot that separated the prime minister's residence and her home office, an area called the TMC gate between 7 and 10 am. In fact, Satwant Singh is said to have told colleagues that he needed to be posted there because it had a toilet nearby and he was suffering from a bout of diarrhea.

Just after 9 am, Mrs. Gandhi walked out of her home towards the TMC gate followed by her entourage – a constable holding her umbrella, her personal attendant and her secretary, R.K. Dhawan. As soon as she approached the gate to step into her office boundary, Beant Singh, a member of her security team for nine years, fired five rounds from his service revolver while Satwant, with an SAF carbine, fired 25 shots at her, which brought her down instantly. Eye-witnesses said that after the shooting, both men threw down their arms and said, 'We have done what we had to do; now you do what you have to.'

As her aides rushed her to the All India Institute of Medical Sciences (AIIMS) where they tried to revive her, the Indo-Tibetan Border Police (ITBP) took the two assailants into custody. While in custody, they shot dead Beant Singh and injured Satwant Singh – a fact that was not taken much cognizance of. Case files reveal that even the court documents barely mention the killing of Beant Singh though they do mention that it was ITBP inspector Tersem Singh who asked the two men to be taken into the guard room. Eye-witnesses say that soon after they heard a round of firing from which Satwant emerged seriously hurt, and Beant, dead. Later in its 1988 order, the Supreme Court recorded that action was asked for against the ITBP personnel but it stopped short of asking for criminal proceedings or an FIR for Beant's shooting. But this was much later. At that moment in 1984 no one had any patience to probe these details or examine the propriety of such an action. People were angry and moved by Mrs. Gandhi's ominous words just one day before her killing: 'I don't mind if my life goes in the service of the nation. If I die today, every drop of my blood will invigorate the nation.'

The news about the shooting (the confirmation of her death would come late in the afternoon), was relayed on the police wireless at 9.23 am. At about 10.30 am, just an hour and a half after the assassination, a junior official at the Directorate General of Supply and Disposal Unit met his colleague, Kehar Singh, and asked him if he had heard anything about Indira Gandhi. Kehar Singh, the 50-year-old uncle of Beant, was reported as saying, 'Whosoever would take confrontation with the *Panth*(s) he would meet the same fate.' Five years later when he was pleading for mercy in the Supreme Court, these words would be held against him. The judges found that these appeared to be the words of someone who had prior knowledge of the assassination plot.

What really sealed Kehar Singh's fate as an accomplice to the prime minister's assassination was the testimony by Beant Singh's wife Bimla Khalsa. Bimla revealed how just 10 days before the assassination, Kehar and Beant Singh made a visit to the Golden Temple. In her statement, she told prosecutors that the two of them went through a kind of purification rite called the *Amrit Chakhna* ceremony at the Golden Temple. On their return, she said, they started behaving in an odd manner and stayed away from the wives. Bimla also told the police that these rituals began after Operation Bluestar, and also involved visits to another gurdwara at Moti Bagh where they heard provocative speeches. She became suspicious, when during Kehar Singh's visits to their home, they would talk about the damage that was done to the Golden Temple, but immediately stop talking when she entered the room. Beant Singh had also apparently told his wife that he would become a 'martyr' but that she and the family would be taken care of.

Bimla Khalsa later became a hostile witness but it was too late by then. The court held the fact that Beant Singh's *kada* or bangle and ring were found in Kehar Singh's home, showed how close he and Kehar Singh were. As a result, the court concluded that Kehar Singh was a 'bigot' who had convinced Beant Singh to assassinate Indira Gandhi.

The fact that Mrs. Gandhi's killers were Sikhs had wide and bloody ramifications for the community. As the news reached Tihar, there was an alert of some Sikh inmates greeting the news of the killing with slogans like '*Khalistan Zindabad*'. To avoid the situation from turning volatile, we swooped in and immediately isolated them. Even before the assassins were brought to jail, Sikh prisoners were very fearful as they faced angry, murderous fellow inmates. I felt terrible seeing what was happening in front of me. The Sikhs are one of the most patriotic and hard-working communities in the country and they were being vilified because of the actions of a few militants. But I do have a theory that I have long held – liberal Sikhs had stayed silent for far too long. Militancy had raged for a long time and if they had taken a stand when it had first started in the early '80s, we would not have reached where we were.

In Tihar, the Sikh inmates who were in jail for terror-related charges were especially scared. So, the first thing we did was to identify and seclude all of them. This meant that those who were lodged in bigger barracks (the ones that could have up to 200 inmates in one) were moved to either individual cells, or those that could accommodate three or five people. Some inmates were also shifted to high-security solitary cells.

Out on the streets, Sikh men and women were being burnt alive with petrol-drenched tyres thrown at them. Soon the Sikh prisoners realized that, despite guards, they were not entirely safe from this retaliation. Desperate SOS messages came to us from the prisoners as horror stories emerged of mobs burning Sikh homes and businesses while the authorities stood as silent spectators to the violence. We gave strict instructions to all security guards for round-the-clock vigilance and ordered that all visits to Sikh inmates had to be supervised. We needed all the manpower we had to protect the Sikh inmates from fellow prisoners and this is why we moved all guards who were previously stationed around the periphery of Tihar, indoors.

Despite this, I cannot say that we were totally immune to the rioting that was happening outside our walls and there were reports of stray incidents of Sikh inmates being beaten up. I am not sure if this was done out of love for Indira Gandhi. I think some used the anti-Sikh atmosphere that was prevalent outside and in the country at the time to simply settle personal scores. As it usually happens in a riot, there are some people who are just looking to benefit from the chaos and in this case some wily, petty criminals used it to defame us. There were a few isolated instances of some Sikhs being struck, but the word went out that we, the jail administrators, were forcing them to cut their hair. Some even complained that we were forcing them to smoke cigarettes, an absolute taboo for Sikhs. Journalists did not believe our denials and these reports were published in newspapers. Even the act of segregation that we did in order to provide them security was misconstrued. The Shiromani Gurdwara Prabandhak Committee (SGPC) wrote to us to ask why we were exploiting Sikh prisoners, which is when we explained to them that most of those who had been complaining against us were petty criminals who had recently found the Sikh cause as a convenient one to benefit themselves.

I could easily spot the troublemakers. Petty criminals who were regulars in Tihar, started growing out their hair and wearing *patkas* or saffron scarves around their heads to look the part of Khalistan supporters. Why? First of all, because it was an exciting, subversive thing to be in jail at the time as it got you plenty of attention from the media. But more importantly, it was about the money. At that time, if you could establish that you were a Khalistani or a Bhindranwale supporter, you could potentially get funds from various supporters abroad. The more notorious you were in jail, the larger the donations came from such support organizations in the UK, US, or Canada. People like Harjinder Singh alias Jhinda, who we knew as a small-time thief went on to become a dreaded Khalistani terrorist in front of my eyes. He was always in and out of jail and never for anything more serious than assaulting someone, petty theft or cheating. Post 1984 he completely re-fashioned himself. We were agog when we heard that he was behind Congress leader Lalit Maken's murder and later in 1986, he was the one who assassinated Army Chief General Arunkumar Shridhar Vaidya, who had led Operation Bluestar. Harjinder may have found his Khalistani cause in Tihar. He was hanged for General Vaidya's murder in a Pune jail in 1992.

We heard rumours that certain families in West Delhi were giving shelter to sympathizers of the Khalistan cause. Of course, nothing was ever proved. Much more tangible was the impact that we saw inside Tihar. I think it is for the first time in the history of criminal justice that the inmates themselves asked to be put in fetters or chains. Initially, when the requests came from those that had to appear in Punjab for legal hearings or other matters, we were intrigued. Then we realized that it was because of the increasing number of militants that were being bumped off as part of the new 'zero tolerance policy' of the state. The textbook modus operandi for this was that when an inmate accused of militancy had to travel to Punjab for a hearing, he would be accompanied by Punjab police officials. It was not unusual to hear that en route the prisoner had 'run away', never to be heard of again. We soon figured that this was code for when they had met with an 'encounter' and eliminated. But if a prisoner submitted a formal request to be put in fetters, the police could not claim he had run away. This request became very common in courts and soon enough encounter killings of this nature also reduced.

Meanwhile, Sikhs in the Delhi Police were rounded up and went through intense grilling sessions to check for any proximity or sympathy towards Khalistani groups. We, in Tihar, also did not want to take any chances. It may be seen as discrimination on the basis of religion these days but all Sikh officers were removed from jail duty in anticipation of Indira Gandhi's two killers being brought to Tihar.

I remember two names clearly – M.S. Ritu, who was the deputy superintendent and another official, B.S. Bhatia – who were removed from their jail duties. Two other Sikh employees were also removed and transferred to a social work department and administration. I am not sure if they knew why they were being moved or whether they were insulted that their loyalty was being questioned, but they submitted to the order without much fuss.

~

Some say that the investigation and trial in the Indira Gandhi assassination case was flawed, as far the law was concerned. In fact, the common belief was that if the victim had been anyone other than Mrs. Gandhi, all the accused would have been acquitted. One major example of this is that one of the shooters, Beant Singh was given instant, self-determined punishment on the spot. With his death, the primary source of the killers' motivation and details of the assassination plot were lost. Further, the police made Beant Singh's wife, Bimla, the star witness so that she would support their claims against Kehar Singh. I was the deputy superintendent (legal) at the time and she would sometimes sit in my office with the investigating officer Assistant Commissioner Rajendra Prasad Kochchar after the case hearings. She would ask him in Punjabi, 'Was that ok?' And he would reply, 'Yes, you spoke very well.' She had already lost her husband and I suppose, giving the testimony the police wanted, put her on their right side of the law.

However, this plan did not work when it came to the case against Sub-Inspector Balbir Singh. His entire conviction was based on the police story that in the first week of September 1984, almost two months before the shooting, Balbir had a sighting that willed him to carry out the killing. Apparently, at his assigned post of duty, which was the front office at the prime minister's residence, he spotted a falcon. The falcon is very symbolic to Sikhs, as the tenth Sikh Guru Gobind Singh was always depicted with a white falcon in his hand.

This was the second instance of religious imagery used in the case with the first being Kehar Singh's baptism of Satwant and Beant with *amrit* at the Golden Temple. The police claimed that when Balbir saw the falcon, he immediately called Beant and the two took a vow right there, that they would avenge the desecration of the Harmandir Sahib.

On the said day, Balbir's duty at the prime minister's house was supposed to begin at 3 pm but when he reported for work, he was told to go to the security lines. Late that night and early next morning, the police raided his house and found what they called 'clinching evidence' – a book on Bhindranwale and a piece of paper that had the following notes:

June 1984
- Army operation
- felt like killing
- Put on duty outside No. 1 S.J. Road against at
- Dalip Singh No. 1 S.J. Road
- Proceeded on leave for 30 days

July 1984
- Dalip & Varinder Singh visited my house
- Dalip took me to Gurbaksh's house where Santa Singh also met
- Dalip Singh & Gurbaksh visited my house Mavalankar Hall
- Went to Ghaziabad
- I visited Gurbaksh Singh's house-for Hemkunt
- I visited Gurbaksh Singh's house
- Back from leave

August 1984
- Met Amarjit Singh & Beant Singh
- Dalip Singh Virender Singh etc. met at Bangla Sahib
- Mavalankar Hall/Gurupurab at Bangla Sahib 3rd Week
- Harpal Singh/Virender
- Beant Singh/Eagle meeting at

- Beant Singh decision to start constructive work PG NO 181

September 1984

- Visited Gurbaksh Singh's house-Dalip & a boy Narinder Singh/Virender
- Leave for 4/5 days 26
- 1000 Visited Gurbaksh's house & learned about the boy

October 1984

- Narinder Singh
- Leave for 4/5 days 22nd - Beant Singh
- Leave for 4 days - Dalip Singh & Mohinder Singh visited 30 - Satwant
- 31 -

It was on the basis of these notes, that a trial court on 26 January 1986 and the high court on 3 December of the same year, confirmed Balbir Singh's death sentence. But the Supreme Court questioned this judgement when they raised a pertinent point: why would a policeman acquainted with the ways of the law, not hide this piece of paper if it made him culpable? They would also cite that the police's star witness, Beant Singh's wife Bimla, never mentioned him as being a part of Kehar and Beant Singh's meetings. These were some of the loopholes in the police case against the assassins that the lower courts had failed to see. These were exposed much later when the Supreme Court confirmed the death sentence for the two men, Kehar and Beant and acquitted Balbir in 1988. But the top court of the land could only undo so much damage by acquitting one man. There were other aspects of the case which were deeply, deeply flawed. Some were very obvious and became the subject of court appeals against the convictions but others, only insiders like me were aware of.

In December 1984, Tihar was preparing itself to receive Kehar, Satwant and Balbir Singh who would stand trial for the most high-profile case in the country. For the first time, we were also going to have a special court set up in the jail premises. A security assessment concluded that the daily to and fro of the accused from Tihar to the court complex for trial was too great of a security threat. When the bodyguards of a prime minister turn on her, the security agencies leave little room for trust. And with the thousands killed in the riots that took place in Delhi after Mrs. Gandhi's assassination, we did not want to take any chances with the safety of the accused either. There was considerable debate about the legal sanctity of such a court. In the Supreme Court, defence counsels like P.N. Lekhi, R.S. Sodhi and Ram Jethmalani argued that a trial inside Tihar is the very 'antithesis of an open trial'. They pointed out that in order to uphold justice and fairness in a trial, the trial itself has to be in an open public space that is accessible to the public and the media, which jails by their very structure, are not.

However, state prosecutors were able to successfully argue that the court building while being in Tihar was not in the main jail complex, but in a separate building. This, they said, was accessible to all outsiders and was separated from the jail quarters by about a kilometer. Of course, in reality, this separate building was actually Jail number 3 and the courtroom was the jail superintendent's office. The accused were brought from Jail number 1 by a van that ferried them back and forth. The court area was nothing like we had ever seen before. For the first time, there were bulletproof enclosures for the Additional Sessions Judge Mahesh Chandra, the witnesses, and the men standing trial. Like other courts in the country, there was space for about 50 members of the public to sit. However, security concerns meant that they would have to apply to attend the trial much in advance. When Kehar Singh's family appealed for a mistrial because the high court had made a jail the justice dispenser, the state pointed out that even in this makeshift space, media representatives were allowed so that there was public accountability.

Even if the state won, you could not dispute that fact that the unusual nature of that courtroom ensured everything was determined by fear. The three accused were so dreaded that we had to keep them in chains even for the short distance from their cells to the courtroom. Putting a prisoner in fetters requires court clearance every single time so there were times when we were unable to get those required permits and immediately, there would be consequences. Twenty-two-year-old Satwant, who was initially very violent would lash out and injure some of our guards. Everyone was terrified that just like the audacious assault on the prime minister, someone would also attack the special court that was trying her killers. The accused were difficult and at times did not even bother to support their own lawyers. At times P.N. Lekhi would be arguing for Satwant Singh's innocence and calling the assassination an international conspiracy, and Satwant would cry out, 'I killed her, I don't know why P.N. Lekhi is saying what he is, but I did kill her!'

Since then, we have had other trials inside the Tihar Court complex, but as this was the first we were figuring things out as we went along. Judge Mahesh Chandra was deeply uncomfortable despite the bulletproof cordon that was made especially for him. It was not a position to envy and he was terrified of facing the defendants because he did not want to appear antagonistic towards them.

When Satwant or Kehar Singh complained in court that they were kept in isolation and that they were mistreated or even beaten (and they often were), Judge Chandra would confer with us before the hearing to discuss what he was going to ask us and what our appropriate answers should be – 'If I say this, then you should say that'. Judge Chandra was under considerable pressure from various quarters. Assistant Commissioner Kochchar used to boast that the judge was chosen so that he would take the prosecution's side and not bother too much about propriety. 'We have a long list of complaints against him,' he once told me, 'If he doesn't give the ruling we want, then we will reveal everything.'

Judge Chandra was under a lot of pressure not just because it was a high-profile case, but also because at times Satwant had been violent. Satwant had attacked guards, when he was not in fetters, so often that Judge Chandra asked us to restrain him when he was addressing the defendants. I remember that there were instances when the defendants wanted to meet the judge separately to perhaps complain about the treatment that they were getting in jail, but he was so scared he would not allow it.

All these transgressions by Satwant were limited to just the initial phase of his incarceration. When he first came to Tihar along with Kehar Singh and Balbir Singh, he was quite a sight to see. The ITBP guard who shot him had pumped at least four-five bullets in him and they were lodged in such critical parts, it was not possible to extract them without killing him. We were handed over a bandaged, angry and very good looking man. At 5 foot 10, he stood taller than most others and had a ruddy complexion – what we Punjabis described as *gabru jawan*. He could not walk because of his injuries and was completely isolated from the other two accused. A special watchtower and police post was created just above these cells. Ward number 1 was cordoned off to everyone else and the jail deputy superintendent was put on his dedicated duty. Because Satwant had a number of surgeries, the ward was more like a hospital room and that there were doctors who would alternate eight-hour shifts. One was Dr. Ashwini Gupta who told us how critical his situation really was. The other doctors were from Deendayal Upadhyay hospital and Ram Manohar Lohia hospital. They would sit by his bedside tending to his medical needs while the jail official would write everything down and send reports to intelligence officials. Even when his injuries healed, no other prisoner could interact with him. The warder would take a group of prisoners who would do the cleaning and leave without exchanging a word with Satwant. It was only when his angry tantrums ended and he stopped assaulting the guards that he could be seen spending time walking or enjoying a game of football with his own security team. Many years later this would become the VIP ward of the jail where people would pay lakhs of rupees to stay. It had six cells and even had a spacious playroom where the VIPs who would come decades after Satwant Singh, would enjoy playing their own games. Because of its seclusion, the other more miserable inmates had no idea how the better off ones lived.

The other two accused were lodged in a different area of the same jail. Kehar Singh, being almost 30 years older than Satwant, looked like any other government babu. Being short in height at 5 feet 4 inches, it was very easy to miss him. He gave us no trouble at all and was like a religious preacher – either reading books of faith or just lying in his bed. If he ever came out of his cell, he would quietly chat with some of the guards and then return to his bed. The third, Balbir Singh was quite tall at 5 feet 10 or 5 feet 11 inches but what distinguished him was that he was a talkative fool. He was full of non-stop nonsense and was lodged in ward number 8 of Jail number 1, next to Kehar Singh's cell. In fact, one theory that was widely held, and I believe to be true, was that the only reason that Balbir was caught and convicted by the lower court is because he bragged too much. Otherwise, why would the police cite a vision of a falcon as the motive for Balbir's assassination plan? He would talk incessantly and boasted about everything, from killing Mrs. Gandhi to even threatening her son, Rajiv Gandhi. His loose talk even upset his own family members.

All three men, due to their extraordinary circumstances, were given special privileges when it came to food. Satwant was given a special cook because the Intelligence Bureau (IB) felt his food could be poisoned by other prisoners. They appointed a teenager called Lakhiram to cook separate meals for Satwant. To take further precautions, they also made his doctor and security men taste the food before Satwant could eat it. Lakhiram stayed on in Tihar much after his first assignment was completed. He became a gardener and eventually graduated to becoming the key aide to the director general of prisons, a position he continues to hold. Everyone realized that the boy who could be trusted with India's most wanted, could be trusted with pretty much anything else. The story goes that the 16-year-old was the son of a trusted peon at the Intelligence Bureau office, but in Tihar he grew to be much more. Kiran Bedi, when she was inspector general of Tihar, attached him to her office and gave him the most important task – handling the complaints box in the jail, which was obviously against officials. Lakhiram continues to be a part of the legacy of the 1984 case.

Returning to the main story, Satwant was not the only one who got special treatment. Kehar and Balbir would get the privileged diet that the B-Class prisoners got of milk and eggs and they could have family members bring them items like dry fruits. While other prisoners would have weekly meetings with their family across a mesh, these men were allowed to meet their family members, under supervision, in their individual wards because they were separated from the general prison population due to security concerns.

I clearly remember one occasion when Balbir's sister visited him. She asked him how he was. True to his ways, he wanted to overcompensate for his circumstances by telling her how happy he was. He said that he got good food and that he enjoyed his entire day's routine. She seemed a bit suspicious and he elaborated on the kind of 'good food' he had in jail. 'We get *paneer* and *kheer*, I like that,' he said, and I will never forget what his sister said. '*Tatti kha tu*' (Eat shit), she said, angry at how he was deluding himself. 'If you have forgotten your family and are happy in jail, you deserve to eat shit.'

Guards also supervised Kehar Singh's family visits when his wife and his stepson Rajinder came to see him. These family visits, like the rest of his jail life, were uneventful apart from his constant claims that he was innocent and had been implicated wrongly by the prosecution. The amazing thing is that none of the families abandoned the three accused and continued to visit them throughout their trial and were with them through the entire process to commute their death sentence. Maybe this was because the communities that they came from were sympathetic to the cause that the killers stood for. Whatever their reasons, they never gave up on these men.

There was one incident though with Satwant's father, Trilok Singh, who would often visit his son in jail and even have lunch with him in his cell. On this visit, Trilok was frisked just like all the other visitors and we found opium on him. This was a very serious transgression for which we were duty bound to file an FIR. But Trilok Singh begged and pleaded that it was for his personal consumption and that he had left it in his pocket by mistake. We decided not to pursue the matter because if word got out, it would only undermine our security arrangements. So, we put a lid on the matter. We did not stop Trilok and the other families from bringing home food for these three men, but took greater care to search all the items they brought. Some may say that what was the need for Indira's killers to get fancy items such as dry fruits from home, but in prison the underlying belief is to strive for reform and home-cooked food was a key to that. The idea was that if an inmate received something from home, he would see the love of his family and this may lead to a positive impact on his mental health. The hope was that it would inspire them to be a kind of person who would have freedom to be with that loving family and to not commit any further crimes. This belief may have eroded now in many prisons but it is what prison officers are taught.

~

All the reformative measures in the world, however, could not save Satwant and Kehar Singh from the gallows. In Balbir Singh's case, the Supreme Court finally stepped in when they said of him:

> Accused is not a rustic person. He is a Sub-Inspector of Police with several years of service to his credit. He must have investigated so many crimes. He must have anticipated the danger of carrying incriminating document when he was already suspected to be a party to the deadly conspiracy. Unable to compromise myself with any reason. I sought the assistance of the learned Additional Solicitor General. He too could not give any explanation. Indeed, nobody

> could offer even a plausible explanation for this unusual conduct attributed to the accused. To my mind, to say that the absconding accused-Sub Inspector was found at a public place in the national capital with an incriminating document which may take him to gallows is to insult the understanding, if not the intelligence, of police force of this country.

And just like that, despite his treacherous threats to kill the prime minister of this country, Balbir Singh was released. I can tell you that the IB was very uncomfortable with the idea of someone who had threatened the new prime minister, Rajiv Gandhi, being released. So they got ACP Kochchar to coordinate his movements from that August day in 1988 when the Supreme Court released him from Tihar. I know this because when I asked why they were bothered with such details, ACP Kochchar confirmed that it was because the Prime Minister's office was afraid Balbir would head there directly once he was released from jail. Nothing as dramatic happened, but I am sure Balbir had the IB following him for a long time afterwards.

That same year, and just before 25-year-old Satwant's mental health started to decline, he got married to a woman in Punjab called Surinder Kaur. The man who had sprayed the prime minister with bullets was apparently considered to be an eligible husband by some. Surinder Kaur had apparently fought with her parents to marry his photograph. I discovered this during one of our conversations by which time Satwant's volatile temper had cooled and did not have to be cuffed anymore. He told me his father had organized the wedding at a gurdwara and used his photograph as a proxy for him.

'Why did you allow him to do that?' I asked Satwant.

'He (my father) said to me that she refuses to marry anyone else other than you.' Satwant added, 'You have to agree that she's very bold to want to marry me despite knowing my future.'

Soon after, as the inevitability of the hanging became apparent, Satwant started sinking. Kehar Singh's family kept pushing one mercy petition after another but Satwant said only God had the authority to judge him and no one else. As Kehar's family went from the home ministry to the president pushing for mercy, Satwant grew quieter and hardly ate. The date for hanging kept changing as their petitions were accepted initially only to be rejected later. We could see that by now, Satwant was mentally not stable.

On the designated day of 6 January 1989, the same two men who had abused Judge Mahesh Chandra for sentencing them to death could not be recognized. Kehar Singh had read his religious scriptures and asked me, as the legal officer, if anything could be done to save him. I think he nursed some hope until the last minute that there may be an intervention on his behalf. Satwant Singh said no such thing but both were shivering, I think more from fear than the cold, winter morning. I remember the last black look on their faces and then, they were gone suddenly.

Once again, the government decided that their bodies should not be handed over to the families. Their last rites had to be done according to their Sikh beliefs. Rules dictate that a cremation can only take place in a designated area. So we came up with a plan (it is quite remarkable how the government can be innovative in its thinking when it wants to be). We got in touch with the Municipal Corporation and quickly got a piece of land next to Jail number 3 declared as a cremation ground. The bodies were then cremated with dignity. To soften the blow of not being present at the cremation, we organized a trip to Haridwar for the families. They were accompanied by a senior police officer and the jail deputy superintendent – I really do think that this went a long way in helping the families make peace with the two men's end.

My wife taught at a Sikh school and this particular case impacted her greatly. She was terrified that I may be facing threats from Khalistan sympathizers. Her colleagues would ask for details of what was happening to Satwant and Kehar in prison. I did not like talking about it and this did not ease her concerns. Apart from General Vaidya, there were many others, like Congress leader Lalit Maken, who had been killed by Sikh militants. There were some reports that the IB was tracking my daily movements because they believed that some jail employees sympathized with Khalistan supporters. The Akal Takht declared Satwant Singh and Kehar Singh as *shaheeds* or martyrs and in Tihar's history they would go down as the men who shouted *'Jo Bole So Nihal'*, as they breathed their last.

DEATH IN CUSTODY

> Prisoners are peculiarly and doubly handicapped. For one thing, most prisoners belong to the weaker segment, in poverty, literacy, social status and the like. Secondly, the prison house is a walled-off world which is incommunicado for the human world, with the result that the bonded inmates are invisible, their voice inaudible, their injustice unheeded.
>
> – Justice Krishna Iyer, 1980

By now the world of Tihar is perhaps a bit more familiar to you. If there was a list to be made of the ironies, of the physical manifestations of the oxymorons of jail life, I would tire of just listing them out one by one. Take for example Sunil Batra, the man behind the landmark 1978 judgement on torture in India, and the reason why solitary confinement is banned by Supreme Court. Did you know he was a torturer himself? Or that decades ago, we paid dearly for the fact that industrialist Rajan Pillai died in our custody, but have still failed to take any substantive measures against future custodial deaths in Tihar? So much so that the rapists and murderers in one of the most heinous crimes in recent times, the 2012 'Nirbhaya' case, were left with other inmates, where there was a possibility of them being lynched. This also led to the prime accused Ram Singh dying in Tihar under suspicious circumstances.

But here I am getting ahead of myself. While the Sunil Batra incident took place much before I joined Tihar – as the one person who directly dealt with complaints and was a part of the justice process and as someone who has been forced to resort to violence to establish order – I have not been blind to the often ludicrous circumstances that surround us. The most memorable one when it comes to torture and mistreatment is the case of Sunil Batra. I have mentioned him earlier too, as part of the brat pack that hung out with Charles Sobhraj, but to remind you, Sunil Batra was the entitled son of a rich, antiques dealer from the upscale neighbourhood of Delhi, Sundar Nagar. He landed in Tihar jail because of an armed robbery in 1973 that went horribly wrong and resulted in the death of two people. Batra, who was 27-years-old then, was sentenced to death and packed off to a solitary cell. But what he did next changed the course of not just his life, but that of all prisoners on death row.

In 1977, from the confines of his cell, Sunil Batra wrote a letter to the Supreme Court that Justice Iyer converted into a petition. Many prisoners write letters to judges and courts but a majority of these just get lost in the backlog of cases. It was happenstance that Justice Iyer had served as a minister of jails in the first government in Kerala and prison reform was an area he was familiar with, so he took Sunil Batra's letter very seriously. In fact, his tenure saw some of the most progressive judgements being passed. He set up a special inquiry to decide the larger question of whether solitary confinement was a just punishment or was it detrimental to the purpose of reform? The case was crucial because Justice Iyer got personally involved. It meant that for the first and only time, in the history of our jails, that Supreme Court judges came to Tihar to see if the conditions were indeed as bad as they were made out to be.

However, when Justice M.H. Beg, Justice P.S. Kailasam and Justice V.R. Krishna Iyer visited Tihar on 23 January 1978, they found that it was not as much of a 'dungeon' as they had been told. While there was no window, bed or any other furniture in the cells they noted that enough sunshine streamed through a ventilator with iron bars. There was no bathroom but there was water and sanitary fittings in the room and they found that Sunil Batra, if he wanted, could communicate with other inmates through the iron bars. Even so, when the justices or judge brothers found that most prisoners preferred physical punishment to solitary confinement, they ruled that it no longer be enforced on Sunil Batra or others as it was no less than torture. This became the foundation of the landmark ruling against solitary confinement. While there is no doubt that solitary confinement continues to be imposed in various jails, it is not legal and prisoners have a provision to complain against it.

This was only the beginning of Sunil Batra's activism. Having interacted with the top judges of the country and tasting success, he wrote another letter a year later, in 1979. In this, he wrote about the horror that was perpetrated on another prisoner, Prem Chand. On 26 August 1979, Prem Chand was taken to Lady Irwin hospital because he was bleeding profusely. The doctor on duty found there was an anal rupture, which the accompanying prison officials initially tried to pass off as an accident caused by Prem Chand's drug addiction. However, the doctor found this explanation implausible and had to perform a surgery to fix the tear. When the complaint reached the Supreme Court, it became another petition that was probed by court-appointed investigators Y.S. Chitale and Mukul Mudgal, who would later go on to become a high-profile judge. Jail officials tried their best to suppress the truth. Besides the 'fall' story, they suggested Prem Chand could have been suffering from piles and even tried to intimidate him to go along with their version of the story but eventually the truth did emerge. According to the Supreme Court judgement, Warder Magger Singh had inserted an iron rod inside Prem Chand's anus because he wanted a bribe for allowing visitors which the prisoner could not afford to give. The sadistic nature of this violation shocked everyone – how wrong could things be inside prisons that not only was this cruel act committed, but Magger Singh had also found support from other prison officials who had tried to cover up his crime. The judges conducting the probe thanked Batra who was then serving a death sentence (later commuted to a life sentence) for raising his voice against this atrocity, forcing the Supreme Court to state in 1979, 'Prisoners are persons not animals, and to punish the deviant "guardians" of the prison system where they go berserk and defile the dignity of the human inmate.'

This case was a turning point as we were forced to confront the torture that took place inside jails. The court asked for handbooks to be published in regional languages which would educate prisoners about their rights. Judicial officers woke up to the other forms of torture which may not have been as blatant as what Magger Singh had done, but still caused considerable pain and humiliation, like transfers to distant prisons where no one could visit, or really humiliating labour like only cleaning faeces or sleeping next to it. They realized that British norms like whipping were still a part of some state jail manuals such as Punjab. These archaic rules allowed up to 30 stripes in the buttocks and up to 15 stripes to juveniles. This was a preferred mode of physical discipline amongst certain jailers and in 1971, they whipped an inmate to death.

But despite the Supreme Court order, torture and assaults on prisoners still exist. The irony is that in jail, often the saviour can be the perpetrator. Barely a year after the landmark Sunil Batra judgement that put jail authorities on the alert, another man serving a life sentence, Rakesh Kaushik, wrote to the courts that he was being mistreated by a gang of prisoners led by Charles Sobhraj, and these men were being supported by the jail superintendent and other officials. It is always the ones serving a life sentence who fight such cases, because unlike the short-stay inmates they have everything to lose. The Supreme Court appointed Subodh Markandey, a well-known lawyer to visit Tihar to get to the bottom of Rakesh Kaushik's list of complaints, which included fraternizing with jail officials to sodomizing young boys and using drugs. Jail officials did their best to make Markandey's job difficult, from stopping his entry to even stealing his briefcase. But Markandey persisted and carried out his investigation. His findings were shocking. The very man who had championed the cause of tortured prisoners was using two minor boys as sex slaves. At that time, there was a separate area in Tihar for juvenile offenders. However, Markandey's report found that 30-year-old Sunil Batra had managed to sneak in a knife into his room and used it to threaten, attack and intimidate others including two teenagers. One of the boys was, 'forcibly dragged and sodomy was committed on him by Sunil Batra.' When the Jail Superintendent B.L. Vij was asked what two minor boys were doing in Sunil Batra's cell (which was fitted with a television), he admitted that 'the two persons were given to him (Batra) for company.' He was asked whether they were 'put to homosexual use', to which he replied in the negative even though Rakesh Kaushik had written to the Supreme Court about alleged acts of sodomy being carried out against minors in Tihar.

The report also quotes witnesses who corroborate the allegation that Sunil Batra and the Sobhraj gang collected bribes from inmates at the behest of Vij and his deputy. In return, they had access to a television, radio, tape-recorder, transistor and a record player – all of which were not allowed according to jail rules. Whoever did not comply to their demands, like one prisoner Srinivas Sharma, Batra beat them.

Why did a whistle blower like Sunil Batra turn into a rapist and tormentor? Or was he always like this? I only met him after the Markandey report was published, by when much of Batra's power had been curbed (due to this report) and there were no minor boys in his cell anymore. The likely reason for the two sides of Sunil Batra is that he was an opportunist – he did things which were convenient for him. He raised the issue of solitary confinement because he himself had been placed there and it made him miserable but he clearly found no contradiction in harassing other prisoners when it suited him. The truth is that there is nothing unusual about sodomy in jails. I do not know how Batra managed to bring minors to his cell (prisoners between the ages of 18-21 are housed in a separate jail) in the huge Tihar campus, but I do know that if those two young boys had complained about the sexual assault to jail authorities, they would have been shooed away and told, '*Bhaag yaar, Bhaag* (Get lost. This happens, deal with it).'

Surveys conducted by various non-governmental organizations have revealed that about 50 per cent of young offenders in jail have been sodomized. Those who are stronger, or have been around in jail for a long time, use sodomy as a tool for suppression and power play. I do not know if Sunil Batra was gay because I've seen straight inmates also turn to homosexuality in jail.

This is another reason why the visionary Justice Iyer was a supporter of furloughs or sanctioned holidays from prison. In the same judgement against torture, he identified a big problem being young offenders housed with older ones or undertrials with convicted, hardened criminals. The convicted, especially those serving life sentences like Sunil Batra, had no reason to be on good behaviour as they had nothing to lose. Their frustration, said Justice Iyer, led many to seek sexual gratification through assault. 'Sex is unquestionably the most pertinent issue to the inmates' life behind bars.' And that was why he said the system of furloughs gave them an incentive to be on good behaviour to be able to pursue conjugal relations. In fact, he advocated the release of prisoners on weekends so they could be with their families. Later, when Kiran Bedi was in charge of Tihar in the early '90s, she came up with the controversial idea of having condom vending machines in jail. I mean, are you trying to invite people to sodomize others? That's what it looked like to me and that is why others challenged it in court as well. But by the time the court took up that decision, Kiran Bedi was no longer in charge of Tihar and fortunately, the idea was not implemented.

In 1981, a controversial decision by the Supreme Court commuted Sunil Batra's death sentence to life and some years later, he was freed. He came back to Tihar after practising law for a few years, this time for a drug-related offence. However, his legacy has lived on and is as relevant even today in prisons. Torture doesn't always have to be in the form of physical or sexual assault. More often, it means custodians turning a blind eye to suffering. Justice Iyer may have passed strictures and ordered strict action against Magger Singh decades ago, but the existence of torture today is evident in the rising numbers of custodial deaths. According to the Ministry of Home Affairs, the National Human Rights Commission has recorded 1,674 custodial deaths across the country in 2017–2018. It seems to have got progressively worse. While there were, on average, four custody deaths per day between 2001 and 2010, it has increased to five per day since. The most high-profile, dramatic and controversial custody death was of biscuit baron Rajan Pillai in Tihar in 1995. I was there through it all and remember the money Tihar had to spend to hire top lawyers like K.T.S. Tulsi and Vikas Pahwa to appear before Justice Leila Seth, who conducted a probe into the incident. It was perhaps the most expensive lesson that Tihar has ever learnt.

By the time the chairman of the Britannia group of companies, Rajan Janardan Mohandas Pillai, was arrested by the Delhi Police, we were very familiar with him. We had followed the story of how he had fallen out with his business partner in Singapore who had filed criminal proceedings against him. When the Singapore court found him guilty in April 1995, Rajan Pillai escaped to Delhi. However, Singapore moved quickly to send extradition notices and Interpol arrest warrants against him, which India had to follow. With pressure from Singapore mounting, the government assigned the extradition case to Judge M.C. Mehta who issued non-bailable warrant against him. On 3 June 1995, after a three-month chase, the business tycoon was arrested from room 1086 at the Le Meridien Hotel in the heart of the Capital. At the time of his arrest, they recovered medicines and alcohol in his hotel room. This was crucial information but for some reason did not feature in his records as it should have.

Rajan Pillai was produced before the magistrate, M.C. Mehta, who was to decide on his extradition the next morning. At this time

Pillai's lawyers produced a certificate from Apollo Hospital stating that he needed medical supervision as he was suffering from alcohol-related liver cirrhosis. More importantly, the note mentioned, just one day before he had passed blood with his stool and also vomited blood, which meant that he was in a critical condition. The medical note warned that if he was not provided with proper treatment, the consequences 'could be fatal'. The note further advised that he be taken to Escorts Hospital for a laser surgery that was required.

Justice Mehta sent Pillai to jail but wrote an urgent letter to the Resident Medical Officer (RMO) to ask if Tihar could look after Pillai and asked the Central Bureau of Investigation (CBI) what they thought of this medical application. He also instructed Tihar to take care of Pillai's medical problems, while awaiting the RMO's full report by the next day.

Everybody in Tihar loves to see a rich inmate joining the prison because it gives them an opportunity to earn money by selling jail facilities. But the 48-year-old Pillai was unlike the rich inmates that we were used to. There was none of the arrogance that usually accompanies the rich and powerful. In fact, he was quiet and a bit submissive. His lawyers, who had an interview with him in jail that day, noted that he was really dejected. Little did they know then how quickly things were going to spiral out of control.

The letter that Judge Mehta had sent for the Tihar RMO never reached him because the person sending it did not treat it as urgent and sent it via a courier, instead of delivering it in person. To make matters worse, the doctor on duty that usually checks new inmates was not present when Pillai was brought in, and so crucial information about his health and weight was not recorded at all.

The next morning, Judge Mehta still had no update from the Tihar doctors and the CBI was not willing to accept any suggestion of poor health as an excuse. They had seen too many crooked politicians and other VIPs successfully using 'medical issues' to evade prison and go to hospitals instead. The CBI officials told the court that Pillai had been drinking at the time of his arrest so the medical note suggesting that he needed treatment at Escorts Hospital was not 'in good faith'. Responding to this, Pillai's lawyers produced his medical reports which showed he had had two life-threatening episodes just three years ago and had to have 10 sclerotherapies (treatment for internal bleeding that impacts eyes). But the judge wanted independent medical advice, which he was hoping the RMO would give him, and so put his decision off until the next day (6 July) and sent Pillai back to Tihar. It was his misfortune that by the time Pillai reached Tihar from court it was five in the evening, which meant the resident doctor had left for the day – once again his physical condition was not checked to verify if what his doctors were claiming to be a precarious life-threatening state was true.

By 6 July, it had been three days since Rajan Pillai had been in custody. In these three days he had not had his prescribed medicines because he had not been examined. The jail authorities admitted in their report to the judge, they didn't have the means to treat liver cirrhosis but they said that it was available in government hospitals like AIIMS. Judge Mehta refused Rajan Pillai's application for a private hospital examination and sent him to Tihar until 11 July, but allowed him to take his medicines. He said, 'professional and morally bound doctors at the jail hospital and the easily accessible court will always be concerned about the permissible and required medical treatment.'

That evening when Rajan Pillai went to his assigned ward 9 in Jail number 4, he was visibly distressed. I heard that he had started shivering in court, so the judge had reiterated his order for proper medical care to be given to him by the doctor at Tihar. The RMO had still not provided an independent assessment of his condition because he claims he never got the letter asking him to. Another inmate, George Kutty, who was from Pillai's home state of Kerala, gave him a *lungi* and bottled water and showed him a cement platform to sleep on. Kutty later recalled that at this point Pillai looked very unwell. After the lock-in, none of us had access to him, but the next morning, during lock-out, guards found Pillai lying on that same cement platform Kutty had showed him. Other inmates told us about how Pillai had been restless all through the night and that his body had became swollen. Another talked of how he repeatedly went to the toilet barefoot, and another saw white spots below his knees. But no one called for help because they took it to be the discomfort of a man new to prison.

When we found him lying on the cement platform, Pillai was in a bad shape and had very high fever. But he was simply taken to the jail doctor instead of a hospital. The jail doctor gave him a calmpose injection which is often used to treat anxiety in new prisoners. There was no attempt to find out his history even though the court had made a special mention of his medical issues. It was only when his lawyer, Pradeep Dewan, came to see him after 4 in the afternoon on 7 July, that he demanded Pillai be taken to a proper hospital.

There have been many theories about how and why Rajan Pillai died, but I believe Tihar's apathy and lack of attention killed him. Despite being informed in court just a day before that the government hospital attached to Tihar, Deen Dayal Upadhyay Hospital (DDUH), was not equipped to deal with liver cirrhosis, the jail authorities still sent him there when his lawyer demanded medical attention on noticing Pillai's high fever. If only someone had cared enough to ensure that Pillai had undergone a medical examination by the Tihar doctor. More precious time was lost when we finally took Pillai to hospital because there was no ambulance available. A desperate Dewan even offered his own car, but we rejected it saying that it went against procedure. To make matters worse, there was no armed police at hand to escort the prisoner to hospital. In total, there was a delay of at least two hours in getting Rajan Pillai to hospital – two hours that proved critical. The stretcher carrying Pillai was placed on the floor in the ambulance and he began bleeding from the mouth en route. On reaching the hospital, no one informed the doctors on call that Pillai had liver cirrhosis and so the doctors kept trying in vain to revive him. At 8.30 pm, Rajan Pillai was declared dead. A post-mortem report said he died because of ruptured esophagal varices, which basically means that enlarged veins in the throat and stomach blocked his airway – a complication of advanced stage of cirrhosis.

No one person was responsible for Pillai's death but a series of failures at every stage. According to me, the biggest culprit was the rule that every inmate needs to be taken to DDUH because it is the closest to Tihar. Because of first hand experience I can say with confidence that even if a healthy person goes to DDUH for a few hours, they will fall sick. Of course, another terrible mistake was the failure of the jail officials to pay attention to Pillai's medical history. The jail doctor didn't even bother to physically examine him despite being told that he had vomited blood. If he had, he would have known that Pillai had psoriasis all over his body and would have sent him to hospital much earlier. Perhaps he would have also given the doctors at DDUH all the information they needed to treat Pillai in a timely manner. But no one cared enough to do the right thing. No one bothered that the original report in front of judge had clearly stated that patients with medical case histories like Pillai could only be handled by AIIMS. Albeit, in my view, the prison administration's lethargic approach for medical treatment of Pillai was not entirely unfounded, as every influential prisoner pretends to be ill while being sent to the jail, and is ready to pay hefty bribe for admission in the jail hospital or any hospital outside.

As you can imagine, the media went crazy with this story. It was splashed all across newspapers and magazines. Thank god there was no 24x7 TV channels at the time but Pillai's death became very political. His widow, Nina, alleged there was an international conspiracy to eliminate her husband and so two probes were set up to investigate his death soon after. The CBI conducted one probe while the former Chief Justice of Himachal Pradesh High Court, Justice Leila Seth was also asked to set up an inquiry. What complicated the matter was that a few prisoners reported they had seen certain jail officials (including one Mahavir Singh) beating Pillai on 4 July, the first day he came to Tihar. Rajinder Singh and two other prisoners testified that they saw Pillai being held down by jail officials while the jail superintendent punched him. To be honest, jail officers beating up convicts is not an uncommon sight, but there are some who enjoy swimming in troubled waters. Rajinder Singh was one of them and used Pillai's death as an opportunity to take advantage of the situation to make things worse for Tihar. But Justice Leila Seth could not determine whether Rajinder Singh or any of the others had actually witnessed such a beating.

At the end of it, even Nina Pillai could not corroborate the theory that she had floated of an international conspiracy to kill her husband. In her testimony, she was unable to name anybody and provide specifics and witnesses so the entire probe needlessly cost us a lot. Many lakhs had to be spent by us to pay lawyers like K.T.S. Tulsi, Vikas Pahwa and others, who had been hired by the government to appear on Tihar's behalf. I know the details because as the legal officer of Tihar, I had to clear the bills myself. After two years, in 1997, the Leila Seth Commission of Inquiry found the doctors and jail officials guilty. However, they never faced any serious consequences. They were issued chargesheets but the inquiries did not lead to anything and they were then let off. In 2011, the Delhi High Court awarded Rs 10 lakh in compensation to Pillai's family which they gave to charity.

Rajan Pillai's death changed the state of amenities in Tihar forever. And while the delivery of justice was slow, the spotlight stayed on the issue because of Pillai's high-profile background. Three years later in 1998, MPs from Pillai's home state Kerala continued to mount pressure on the government which led to then Home Minister L.K. Advani assuring Parliament that no other prisoner would die because of lack of facilities like Pillai had. Advani directed the number of jail doctors be increased from the sanctioned 16 to 110, our paramedic staff went from 80 to 200 and all of them were rostered for shifts to cover Tihar's inmates round-the-clock. Medical checkups of new prisoners is now mandatory to ensure that no existing medical condition of new arrival goes undetected. During a Parliament discussion in 1998, L.K. Advani committed that the government would make 'systemic changes so that a thing like this does not happen in the future.' But of course, it did.

~

Are there some who deserve to be tortured? Of course not, never in any circumstances. But what about those who had done something so cruel and evil that even the judge uses language such as 'hair-raising, beastly, unparalleled behaviour', when sentencing them. I am fast forwarding 15 years to December 2012 when the country was enraged by a 23-year-old paramedic's brutal rape in the national capital.

There was just reason for the anger that greeted Ram Singh, Mukesh, Vinay, Akshay and Pawan – the five men, who along with a juvenile, gang-raped and brutalized the young woman and her boyfriend on a moving bus on 16 December 2012. Even if we ignore the angry headlines and the protests of people on the streets and just go by the objective details of the judgement, it is one of the most heinous crimes to have been committed in India.

On that cold December night, the young woman and her boyfriend had watched the Oscar winning movie *Life of Pi* at a theatre at Select City Mall in Saket. Post the movie, they were looking for transport to Dwarka and were offered a ride by a commercial bus which had only five men (including the bus driver). Thirty-three-year-old Ram Singh, a widower, was the driver of the chartered bus and also the oldest of the group. When the paramedic and her friend got on, they paid 10 rupees each as fare and the bus made its way past Delhi traffic. Suddenly the lights inside the bus went off. Soon after, the men began harassing the two passengers, asking them what they were doing out so late at night. When the boyfriend protested, the men slapped and stripped him and then beat him with iron rods. After taking away both their phones and wallets, Ram Singh, Akshay and the juvenile took the girl to the back of the bus and raped her one by one. Pawan and Kalyan held her boyfriend down while Mukesh drove the bus around the city, without anyone noticing anything strange. Earlier that evening, the same men had robbed a man who had already reported the bus and his assailants to the police helpline.

The three continued to assault and gang-rape the girl, with Mukesh even taking a break from driving to do so, while two of them beat her friend. They bit her entire body, including her breasts, arms, thighs, and her face. Finally, they took iron rods and inserted it into her vagina and anus. Those that didn't have rods, inserted their hands, and as if scripting their own grotesque mode of torture, pulled her intestines out. When doctors would examine her later, they would discover that her intestines was perforated, splayed, and cut open due to these actions. The courts would cite this as the reason for giving the perpetrators the death penalty, saying they were 'exhibiting extreme mental perversion not worthy of human condonation' because who would drag a woman with her innards hanging out, by her hair from the back of the bus to the front because the back door was jammed. In this naked, spiked to smithereens state, the men threw out both the girl and her boyfriend on the road and tried to run them over. It was only because the boy who still had some strength left, managed to pull her away from the bus tyres, that she survived. Her injuries were so severe that she died less than two weeks later. However, she managed to give her statement before dying and this led to the five men arriving in our custody in Tihar.

At that time, Vimla Mehra was the director general of prisons, Delhi. The IPS officer had earlier run the Crime Against Women Cell for many years and had witnessed first-hand horrific cases of violence against women, but this case affected her very deeply. She would get overwhelmed with emotion and break down and cry. One of the first decisions, Vimla Mehra took about the five men (the juvenile went to a home meant for underage offenders), was to place them in a regular jail. I had argued for a high-security ward because they were at great risk from the general population in Tihar as there was a lot of anger against these men. In the interest of their safety, it would have been prudent to separate them from the other prisoners.

However, Vimla Mehra was adamant. She sent Pawan and Vinay to the young adults' jail because they were under the age of 21, Ram Singh was sent to Jail number 3 and Mukesh and Akshay to Jail number 4 – all regular jails.

While I was definitely not sympathetic towards these men, I wanted to follow due process. 'What if somebody kills them,' I asked. 'Let them,' she said, 'What do you have to do with it.' It wasn't a stray comment. Apart from the heinous act that he had carried out, Ram Singh's physical appearance of close-set eyes, receding hairline and bony face, ensured that there was little sympathy for him. It seemed as if every day the press would discover new details about his life at a slum settlement called Ravi Das Camp, and people had new reasons to hate him. The slum was set in a crowded part of South Delhi called Munirka and ironically the most distinguishing feature about the area is a prominent police station. Many social commentators would attribute Singh's loud wanton ways – his drinking and the words he uttered to the 23-year-old before he assaulted her – to the influence of the miserable surroundings of Ravi Das Camp. Public opinion was strongly against these men and there were daily protests for the authorities to take action against them. At our review meetings, if we tried to discuss special arrangements required for their security, Vimla Mehra would turn it down. In fact, she would at times get a little carried away. She made it clear that in this particular case, if they faced the ire of a jail mob, she was fine with it.

As a result of this attitude, there were a few procedures which were overlooked. The first being the Test Identification Parade (TIP), which is an important evidence gathering process. This takes place in the day time and in front of a judge and not the police. But in this case, it happened after 7.30 pm. The boyfriend, who was treated for broken ribs, was brought in to identify Ram Singh and the others. It was not just the timing which was odd and against procedure, the police were also present, a move which can be interpreted as intimidatory and therefore illegal. There was no subtlety in the way it was done either. The station house officer of Vasant Vihar, Anil

Sharma, was present and moving freely while the formal TIP was completed at a time when the accused should have been locked up for the night. I had not seen such a great violation of rules for any prior cases. But then again, I do not know how many men like Ram Singh I had encountered. As law officer I was present during the TIP.

I took this opportunity to speak to Ram Singh one-on-one. It was something that was niggling my mind. 'Why did you do it?' His answer was matter of fact, almost as if he had merely committed a petty theft.

'We were drunk. Where we live, people are not good.'

'Why, it is your home,' I retorted.

'No, good people are not there. They drink and they curse and I have also become like that, like an animal.'

Speaking specifically about the incident, Ram Singh said the couple had sat at the back of the bus and were kissing which 'agitated' all five of them. The other four including Ram Singh's brother, Mukesh, all unanimously said that none of it would have happened if Ram Singh had not initiated the attack and encouraged the others to join him in brutalizing the young woman. Mukesh said if he had not gone along with it, he was sure that Ram Singh would have beaten him. However, we do not know if the courts would have made a distinction between Ram Singh's role and that of the other men.

Less than three months after he was in judicial custody, 11 March 2013 to be precise, the alarm went off at Tihar. When I heard the news, I rushed to jail to find Ram Singh's body hanging. There is no written evidence anywhere, and I do not have a copy of the post-mortem report, but I do believe that Ram Singh did not commit suicide. For one, his viscera report which I saw showed alcohol content in his body. This should have raised suspicion and made the police register an FIR – how could an inmate get access to alcohol? The second reason as to why his 'suicide' was suspicious was that the ceiling where he had been hung from was at least 12 feet high. Considering that there were three other inmates in the same cell as him, I felt that it was not possible that Ram Singh had managed to quietly hang himself from such a high ceiling. He had apparently used his pyjama cord to hang himself. Next to him was a plastic bucket. To me it looked like he was made to drink and then hanged. In fact, his body had injuries too. A sub-divisional magistrate (SDM) inquiry was ordered to probe the suicide but I knew an SDM would not cry murder even if it happened in front of his very eyes. The SDM is too involved with the current jail system to give an adverse report against jail officials. So I knew that this was not going to lead to anything. Ram Singh's lawyers cried foul, and his father told the media it was not possible that his son could lift himself up to the rope because he had a bad arm. But who wanted to hear all this? At that time no one was interested to know why Ram Singh's death was suspicious. They wanted to see him dead and if it had been done in jail, then so be it.

When I think about that case, I am sometimes amazed how the other four men survived. I know that they were severely beaten when they first came to jail, but how did they escape being lynched? The SDM's report came as no surprise – it concluded that Ram Singh's death was indeed a suicide. I believe Ram Singh's cell mates were allowed to murder him.

Sometime later, in July 2013, Vimla Mehra allowed a BBC crew to film a documentary about the December 2012 gang-rape and death of the young girl. The film crew shot inside the jail and even managed to gain access to interview Mukesh. Titled *India's Daughter*, the documentary was filmed soon after Ram Singh's death and was eventually released in 2015. I had deep reservations regarding the documentary and the access the filmmakers were allowed. I shared my views with the director general that the local media and press would be very upset with a foreign team getting unprecedented access. Also, I knew that the documentary would not make us look good. My worst fears were confirmed when excerpts of Mukesh's interview were released:

> A decent girl will not roam around at nine o'clock at night. A girl is far more responsible for rape than a boy.

> Housework and housekeeping is for girls, not roaming in discos and bars at night doing wrong things, wearing wrong clothes. About 20 per cent of girls are good... When being raped, she should not fight back. She should just be silent and allow the rape. Then they would have dropped her off after "doing her", and only hit the boy. The death penalty will make things even more dangerous for girls. Now when they rape, they will not leave the girl like we did. They will kill her. Before, they would rape and say, "Leave her, she will not tell anyone." Now when they rape, especially the criminal types, they will just kill the girl. Death.

Before he died, Ram Singh had told me the same thing that Mukesh Singh told the BBC team – the young woman was to blame for her own rape. These were, to put it mildly, very unpopular statements after such a heinous crime and so when the documentary was released there was uproar. Vimla Mehra had allowed them this platform and it became a major controversy which led to the government setting up an inquiry to investigate how and why a film crew was allowed to conduct these interviews inside a jail. By this time Mehra was no longer at Tihar and it became our and especially my headache, as the press officer, to justify it to the new government. It became a major political showdown with debates in Parliament about the issue. Women's groups, politicians, everybody was agitated about both the rapists' views but also with the government for allowing him a platform. The NDA government led by Prime Minister Narendra Modi banned the BBC documentary in India in 2015 and wanted to know just how this crew had got permission.

My fears about this documentary project had come true. I still do not know why Vimla Mehra was so keen to allow the BBC such access inside Tihar. Since then, media interviews which were always limited are now totally off-limits. Ram Singh was soon forgotten but while the juvenile finished his punishment and was freed, Mukesh, Pavan, Vinay and Akshay await their death sentence. Custodial deaths still continue.

AFZAL GURU: THE FINAL ACT

When your workplace is a prison, you learn to keep secrets. Sometimes, secrets are necessary for reform and rehabilitation to help an ex-prisoner adjust to the world outside. For instance, an unspoken rule is that you may share a camaraderie inside jail but if you bump into a former prisoner once they have left jail, you do not assume familiarity. It is not considered polite to remind a person who has done time about their days of incarceration. It is for this reason that I do not accept invitations of weddings or other functions of former prisoners. Even if I saw someone I knew really well, I would avoid him in public. A few months ago I was at Bikaner House, New Delhi for a book launch where I saw industrialist Raj Sethia who had spent time in Tihar for a financial crime fraud. He was in prison at the same time as Sobhraj and the two knew each other well. We both registered each other's presence but even after so many years together, we did not speak to each other because, I feel, he did not want to be reminded that I had been his jailer at one time.

Another secret I keep is the number of people I have indulged with jail fetishes. For example did you know that a common fetish is to eat jail food? Yes, that is right. Some believe that if you are going through a rough patch, and experiencing bad luck in life, all you have to do to fix things, is to eat the food from a jail kitchen. One possible explanation for this is that all other miseries are put into perspective after eating the abominable food from Tihar. But seriously, I have received calls from friends, lawyers and even high court judges who wanted me to organize food from Tihar so that their own lives could become more appetizing. There were others who asked for jail food because their horoscopes apparently said that they would do time in jail at some point in their life. To ward off this predestined misfortune, they would ask us if they could voluntarily spend one night in jail or eat jail food. This fix is supposedly mentioned in *Lal Qitaab*, which is like the 'bible' or even an almanac that some communities in North India use to tackle miseries dictated by our stars.

It is strange when even the most educated are willing to suspend their rational minds for superstition. Besides many judges, there was one bank manager who I remember well. She was in trouble at work because she had given a loan to someone who had defaulted on it. She took someone's advice and came to see me. I could not turn her away because she was sent by a good friend. She came to see me about three times and would not only eat the jail food but also clean cupboards and dust the room! How can anyone believe that this kind of fix will work? By this logic all ex-convicts would be living without a care in the world!

Besides prison food other articles from jail were also believed to have 'healing powers'. The wood used for the hanging plank was highly sought after because it was believed to ward off fear. Some people believe that by placing a piece of this wood in a child's bedroom could help him or her get over nightmares and also stop bedwetting. It could also help a child overcome exam fear. I have been told that many seers sell amulets with soil from a jail because of its supposed extraordinary powers. Whenever someone would ask for water or soil from Tihar, we would go along with it and one of the constables would organize it for them.

But there was one superstition which we, as jail authorities, tried to actively counter. In 2001 we noticed there had been a rise in the number of childbirths in Tihar. As I was compiling the annual statistics, I noticed there were at least 50 women in jail who were pregnant. In many such cases, the women would apply for bail and would get it soon after the birth of the child. The initial assumption was these women wanted to be arrested because they wanted to avail of the jail's fairly decent pre-natal facilities. If you were poor, being in jail was a good option because it meant that you would get regular meals and your medical needs would also be taken care of. While our facilities were far from fancy, some of the poor prisoners would not even have access to the most basic healthcare outside of Tihar.

However, when I chatted with these women, I found another reason why they so badly wanted to remain in Tihar. Many of them held the belief that giving birth in jail would ensure they have a son instead of a daughter. Apparently, this belief finds it roots from the story of the birth of Krishna. According to mythology, Devaki and Vasudeva were imprisoned by her brother, King Kansa, because he knew that one of their children was going to be the cause of his death. Kansa managed to kill their children but when Vishnu reincarnated himself as Krishna and was born in prison as their eighth child, Vasudeva found himself free and managed to swap the baby with a girl child born to Yashoda and Nanda. Thus Krishna survived, grew up as a cowherd and then, as legend has it, slayed the evil Kansa.

This phenomenon of pregnant women purposely trying to get arrested in order to ensure a male child was not at all acceptable to us as it perpetuated the ancient evil of a bias against the girl child. The belief that jail brings forth a male child was so strong that women would get into petty fights or theft in the final stages of their pregnancy. The desperation to have a son drove them to try this as an added measure. We faced the challenge of sending them away. How were we going to convince them? There was not much we could do about it actually other than spread facts. We shared these facts with reporters so that they could write about it and the word would spread. However, this was not that simple because most of the women were from low-income families with little education. Finding that the news reports were not really helping, we pasted these statistics in slums and other areas adjoining the jails. We did everything we could, but it did not have the desired effect.

~

On 3 February 2013, President Pranab Mukherjee rejected Mohammad Afzal Guru's mercy petition. Afzal was sentenced to death for providing logistical support to the men who attacked the Indian Parliament in 2001. All five of the terrorists and seven civilians were killed in this attack, including a woman CRPF officer, a Parliament staffer and a gardener. Afzal Guru was sentenced to death in August 2005 and thus began his long, lonely wait for his end in an isolated ward. Many hanging dates had come and gone – 20 October 2006 was the first chosen day for his execution and it was put off only because of his wife Tabassum's intervention when pleaded with President A.P.J. Abdul Kalam for mercy. President Kalam did not take a decision and his successor, President Pratibha Patil, also let her entire tenure go by without making a decision, even though she pardoned 34 other convicts. Her successor, President Pranab Mukherjee, however, was far more decisive in favour of hanging convicts. According to newspaper reports, out of the 33 prisoners who pleaded for his mercy, he granted it only to two.

Forty-three-year-old Afzal Guru was not one of the lucky ones and to ensure that this time there would not be another intervention by Tabassum or civil society activists, the government kept this decision under wraps. Once the president decides, it becomes our job to implement the hanging and so it was my responsibility to get Afzal Guru's black warrant issued. I did not realize that this was to be my last black warrant and therefore hanging. By now, I was no longer nervous or excited about such occasions. For 32 years, I had seen terrorists, murderers, rapists and yes, even innocent men, being punished. I was meant to be a part of their reform, to correct their wrongs but I no longer had any illusions of doing so. I was just a weary man doing the job that he was assigned to do.

I was well aware of the kind of protests that would be sparked by the news of Afzal's hanging. Well-known writers, academics and other active members of civil society had protested against the death sentence handed to him. We knew the extreme sensitivity of this particular case and therefore the need for secrecy around the actual hanging. The Ministry of Home Affairs was not taking any risks and the files regarding execution were being directly handled by the Lieutenant Governor of Delhi Tejendra Khanna, who was administratively in charge of Tihar and DG (Prisons), with no other officer kept in the loop. A Congress government led by the late chief minister Sheila Dikshit was in power in Delhi so it was not even an issue of sparring with an opposing government at the Centre.

President Mukherjee took this decision to reject the mercy petition on a Sunday and I was put on the job soon after the LG forwarded the file to DG Vimla Mehra. My assignment was to make sure the court issued the black warrant with minimum fuss and so I went to meet Judge I.S. Mehta, who was in charge of Patiala House court. While the exact schedule of events is a little unclear in my memory, I think it was the next working day that I requested to meet Justice Mehta in his chamber. As I have mentioned earlier, judges, however tough they are, hate this part of their job. That's why they have kept the tradition alive of breaking the nib of the pen or throwing away the pen itself that they use to issue the black warrant. Perhaps Justice Mehta had the same apprehension any of us would have. Would Kashmiri terrorists target him for being involved in Afzal's hanging? Would he get security from the government? These were all valid questions that any of us would have asked if we were in his place. I felt for Justice Mehta, who would have his name linked forever with Afzal Guru's hanging.

Justice Mehta assigned 8 February 2013 as the date of Afzal's hanging, which gave us less than four days to prepare. The police intelligence had reviewed the date of hanging and concluded that it would be disastrous to hang him on a Friday. In his home state of Jammu and Kashmir, Afzal's death sentence was an explosive issue and if the news of his hanging came as people headed out for Friday prayers it could lead to a volatile law and order situation in the Valley. Therefore I had to convince Justice Mehta to assign another date. He gave us a black warrant for the next day, 9 February – a Saturday. When I think about it now, I can't miss the coincidence of it all. The first Kashmiri separatist hanged in Tihar was Maqbool Butt and his date of hanging was also changed for the same reason. Maqbool and Afzal had other things in common too, but more about that later.

Every aspect of Afzal Guru's case was controversial. To start with, the Supreme Court itself admitted that Afzal Guru was not part of any terror group, not part of Jaish-e-Mohammed which was behind the Parliament attack. The human rights groups brought that up along with many other inconsistencies as they campaigned against the death sentence. They pointed out how everyone else that had been arrested at the same time as Afzal Guru (Professor S.A.R. Geelani, Shaukat and Navjot Guru) were all set free.

According to the police files, Afzal had never denied that he was in touch with Mohammed – one of the five terrorists killed during the Parliament attack. Call records from a phone that Afzal used showed that he was in touch with Mohammed, from 28 November until the day of the attack, 13 December 2001. However, what Afzal pointed out (and the court did not accept) were details of how that phone was provided to him by the Special Task Force (STF) in Kashmir. According to him, the STF had tortured him from the time he returned to Kashmir from his failed adventure as a separatist in Pakistan. Telling gory tales of how the STF would pick on people like him despite being a surrendered militant as certified by the Border Security Force (BSF), Afzal alleged that he had no choice but to help Mohammed. Afzal named someone called

Davinder Singh, a deputy superintendent of police in the Jammu and Kashmir Special Operations Group. He said his involvement in the entire attack came about because Singh asked him to take Parliament attacker Mohammed to Delhi and to provide him with all the help he needed. This allegation was important because as activists and writers like Arundhati Roy pointed out this was the same officer who dealt with Afzal when he had surrendered as a JKLF militant. Davinder Singh was a traffic policeman in 2013, and is still in the J&K police force. When reporters confronted him, he admitted that he had arrested Afzal but these allegations were never properly addressed by any authorities. Afzal's lawyers continued to maintain that it was police officials like Davinder who had helped to buy the Ambassador car that was later found to be involved in the attack and that is how the phone conversations between him and the terrorist Mohammed came to be. After the car was bought, Afzal said he was asked by Mohammed to go back home to Kashmir which means that he had a peripheral role to play. But he was arrested from a bus stop in Srinagar two days after the Parliament attack and now he was to be hanged.

Activists fought against Afzal's death sentence because the arguments that he put forward did not get much play. They do not figure in the court judgements either because for at least six months into the case, Afzal did not have a lawyer representing his case. The Supreme Court itself admitted that until 17 May 2002, there was no lawyer for Afzal. No lawyer protested against him being paraded in front of TV cameras, no lawyer who objected to the charges of the then draconian anti-terror law called Prevention of Terror Act (POTA), and definitely no lawyer when he signed the pages of confession which despite being made in front of a police officer were upheld by the court. It was this law, POTA, that stated that 'a confession made by a person before a police officer not lower in rank than a Superintendent of Police and recorded by such police officer either in writing or on any mechanical or electronic device shall be admissible in the trial of such person.' More than six months after the attack, counsel Seema Gulati appeared for Afzal, but within a month she excused herself saying she had found another client. The court then appointed counsel Neeraj Bansal to Afzal's case. However, Afzal was not happy with Bansal and gave names of four lawyers he wanted to represent him. But he was told they were all unavailable. Prisoners' rights in India and various judgements like the RD Upadhyay vs State of Andhra Pradesh order in 2006 say that all prisoners have the right to have legal representation and a fair trial. What do you do, however, if lawyers ignore this and choose a sense of patriotism over a matter of legal fairness?

This was when notables like the late Ram Jethmalani, who had helped many others escape the gallows, got involved and pointed out the various loopholes in the police case and basic problems with the prosecution's case. The case against Afzal Guru was under terror or POTA charges which needed clearance from the Centre but in this case it was given by the Delhi Government. Also, Jethmalani argued, the entire case was based on Afzal's 'confession' but they had charged him with plotting the entire conspiracy to attack Parliament. The basic objection was – how can you base conviction and death penalty simply on a confession?

But by now it was too late as the media interviews the police had forced Afzal to give were too ingrained in the public's mind. Afzal's defence team pointed out how permission to tap phones used by Afzal and the attacker was not taken in the proper manner, how POTA which allowed confessions to the police instead of the court, was added at a much later stage, and many other problems in the Evidence Act all related to the use of Afzal's confession despite its retraction. But no one was listening. The trial court and the high court had both accepted the police version that Afzal Guru, who had surrendered as a former militant in 1993, was again recruited in October 2001 to help terrorists plan and execute the attack on the Indian Parliament. This was why the courts believed that Afzal had contacted his cousin Shaukat to organize a place for the terrorists to stay in Delhi and that Afzal and Shaukat provided help to the five terrorists in exchange for 10 lakh rupees. According to the police chargesheet and case documents, the incontestable proof of Afzal's involvement was that he was caught with the money and the laptop, on which fake ID cards were made, which allowed the terrorists access to Parliament. On 5 March 2019, a Supreme Court bench of Justices A.K. Sikri, M.R. Shah and Abdul Nazeer would for the first time acquit six people on death row because they did not get proper legal representation but in 2005, the Supreme Court dismissed the review plea for Afzal Guru by saying,

> The incident, which resulted in heavy casualties, had shaken the entire nation and the collective conscience of the society will only be satisfied if the capital punishment is awarded to the offender. ...The appellant, who is a surrendered militant and who was bent upon repeating the acts of treason against the nation, is a menace to the society and his life should become extinct.

The rules related to a hanging are very clear. We need to inform the family and help them meet the prisoner for a last time. This rule is included in every prison manual across the country and to implement it is the responsibility of the jail superintendent. But between the time that President Pranab Mukherjee dismissed the mercy petition and the date of the hanging we did not have the usual two weeks, but only six days. However, six days was definitely enough time to inform Azfal's family and to allow for a last meeting. He was in a high-security ward and to meet him, his family would have to seek prior permission and then come from Kashmir. While many privileged prisoners were helped by prison officials to meet their visitors in officials' rooms, Afzal Guru being behind the Parliament attack was not offered any such opportunities. His son, Ghalib, was only two-years-old when his father was arrested and did not remember him as a free man.

If they had been told in time, the family could have flown down to see him from Sopore, Kashmir one last time. It is not unusual for a large group of people to come and meet the prisoner before he is hanged. The Supreme Court has now made it mandatory to have a two-week notice period between the rejection of the mercy petition and the hanging for a number of reasons. Foremost among them is that prisoners get time to mentally prepare themselves. They finish their business and do whatever they need to do to be at peace – prepare a will, settle their affairs and meet their loved ones.

On 6 February, three days before the hanging and three days after the president sealed his fate, a letter was sent by speed post by the superintendent of Jail number 3. Addressed to Afzal's wife Tabassum, it said, 'The mercy petition of the convict Sh Mohd Afjal (sic) Guru s/o Habibullah has been rejected by the Honourable President of India. Hence the execution of Sh Mohd Afjal Guru s/o Habibullah has been fixed for 9/02/13 at 8 am in Central Jail Number 3. This is for your information and for further necessary action.' As reported by media, by the time this letter reached Tabassum, there was no action possible for the family.

There are so many threads to Afzal Guru's story and while I only met him only a few times, I, like Justice Mehta, am also inextricably linked to his story. When faced with outrage from civil society about a letter being sent to Afzal's family instead of a phone call, Union Home Secretary R.K. Singh denied any wrongdoing on the government's part, and even claimed that the Kashmir Director General of Police (DGP) Ashok Prasad was informed as per procedure. But the DGP Kashmir's boss, the then Chief Minister Omar Abdullah, could not understand why the Central Government would resort to this level of cruelty, and not inform the family in advance instead of letting them find out via the media. 'I cannot reconcile myself to the fact that his family was not allowed to see him before he was killed or executed. That, to my mind, is the biggest tragedy of this execution,' Omar Abdullah was reported by the Press Trust of India as saying.

~

Home Secretary R.K. Singh, who later became a minister for power in the Narendra Modi government, worked very closely with us in planning the execution. Our first interaction was when a meeting was fixed between the jail authorities and the then Home Minister Sushil Kumar Shinde. My boss Vimla asked me to come along because I was the legal officer. We faced a challenge – Kalu and Fakira, the two hangmen who had pulled the lever for all the executions in Tihar that I had seen, had passed on, and we had nobody to replace them. Hangings were so rare that there was no real need to fill their position. Anyway, we were confident that the job could be done by one of our staffers – all we had to do was to follow the very detailed instructions that are given in the jail manual.

However, Vimla Mehra wanted to make sure that the government was on the same page as us and so we made the trip to North Block to meet the home minister and his team. With only two days left to the date of hanging, we reached the home minister's office shortly after noon. The only ones present for the meeting were Vimla Mehra, Sushil Kumar Shinde, R.K. Singh and myself. Mehra gave them a brief rundown of how we planned to carry out the execution despite the lack of a hangman. Shinde and Singh then asked if we were confident about being able to do so without any glitches and we replied in the affirmative. We pointed out that without old and trusted professionals such as Kalu and Fakira, we could not just bring in anyone new for such a high-profile and confidential case. Both men nodded and gave us the go ahead. This would be the first and the last hanging without a hangman. Shortly after, in January 2014, the Supreme Court gave the Shatrughan Chauhan order, which was basically a petition of 15 people who were on death penalty. The judgement put in strict rules about executions and also made it mandatory to have a post-mortem after the hanging.

There was one more meeting which took place the night before Afzal's hanging. At about 10 pm on Friday, the Home Secretary R.K. Singh summoned Vimla Mehra and me to his home in New Moti Bagh. There was no specific purpose to the meeting, he just wanted to make sure one last time that we could handle the procedures ourselves. The meeting lasted about 10-15 minutes and the thing I remember most about it is that he asked his wife to join us as well. It was probably out of courtesy because a woman officer had come to see him so late at night. With this meeting, the entire operation was now entrusted to us. These rounds of meetings obviously had a great impact on all of us.

Early the next morning when the jail authorities began the practice runs for the hanging, they experienced a major problem. As part of the prison manual's instructions, you have to practice on sandbags. As I said before, you prepare sandbags according to the prisoner's weight and do a check using these. They had conducted this test at 2 am, as a part of the all-night vigil before a hanging. During this test, the rope broke. These ropes, called 'Manila Ropes', are especially brought from Buxar Jail, Bihar. The rope had been procured in 2005 when Afzal was sentenced to death. The many years since had eaten away and weakened the rope. At that time, the deputy superintendent of Jail number 3 took the details of Afzal's height and weight from our records (which are constantly updated) and got another rope made in two days and at a cost of Rs 860 from Bihar. If you ask the rope makers they will tell you how the Ganga flowing nearby gives the right kind of humidity that such a special purpose rope needs. But there had been so many legal interventions and years of delay in Afzal's case that this well treated-custom-made rope had malfunctioned. They were in a state of panic. What if they could not produce the right rope just a few hours before the hanging? If the wrong kind of rope caused an accident like a decapitation, it would be a terrible scandal. So, with a prayer on their lips, they tried again. They slowly lifted the sack, tied it to the noose and then pulled the lever a second time. But it broke again. All this while Afzal was sleeping peacefully. Of course, he must have had some indication as the night before the hanging he was moved from his isolated ward to one with some inmates so that the *phansi kothi* could be prepared. Perhaps, in his heart, he knew that his time was coming to an end.

Unlike all other inmates who went through the ritual of getting their last wish and meal, Afzal was still unaware. Meanwhile, the sandbag exercise was successful in the third attempt.

At 6 am, it was time to tell Afzal of his imminent death. We had seen each other around, and knew of the other, but there had been no conversation between us – until now. I would see him walking with other inmates and reading books of different faiths – Gita, Quran and the Vedas. When he wasn't reading, he was usually doing his prayers – unfailingly five times a day.

'With regret, I have to tell you that today is your hanging,' the superintendent informed him.

'I know, I figured.'

We sat down with him and asked if he wanted tea. As we sipped it slowly, Afzal spoke calmly about his case. He told us he was not a terrorist, and that he was not even a wanted person. All he wanted, he said, was to fight against corruption but 'who listens in India?'

'This was never my fight. I never wanted or even intended to be a Kashmiri separatist. All that I did was to fight against corrupt politicians.'

And then he started singing a song from the 1960s movie *Badal*, *'Apney liye jiye toh kya jiye, tu ji ae dil zamane ke liye.'*

(What's the point of a life lived for ourselves, my heart lives for others).

It is a lovely song picturized on the actor Sanjeev Kumar singing in prison. Like the character in the film, Afzal was telling us that everything he did was for a larger cause. There was no fear in his voice. There was just something about the way Afzal sang it, that I could not help myself. I sang along with him until he stopped and asked for some more tea. Unfortunately, the man who serves tea in prison had already left so this wish of his remained unfulfilled.

The superintendent asked him if he wanted to give a message to those he was leaving behind as we feared there may be riots and acts of violence after his hanging and asked him if he would want to give a message to urge everyone to remain peaceful.

'I see compassion in your eyes. Will you be there at the time of hanging?' he asked.

'Don't worry.'

'Make sure I am not in pain,' he said to the superintendent.

As the prison authorities led him into the *phansi kothi*, my colleagues who had been practicing all night were ready to carry out the act. When Afzal was ready, the staff member who pulled the lever looked towards the superintendent and he nodded as per rules contained in the jail manual.

Two hours later, after doctors certified his time of death, Afzal was buried according to Muslim rites right next to where Maqbool Butt had been buried 30 years ago. Afzal's hand scribbled note written moments before his hanging reached his family in just 26 hours. This time around, the authorities posted the note on Monday, 11 February and it reached the very next day, despite the fact that there was curfew in the Valley, to deal with any kind of backlash.

9/2/2013

Respected family and all the believers.

Asalam u alikum (peace up on you)

I thank almighty that he has chosen me for this stature. From my side, I want to congratulate all the believers. We all should stay with truth and righteousness, and our end must also come on the path of truth and righteousness. My request to my family is that instead of grieving over my end, they should respect the stature I have achieved.

Almighty God is your greatest protector and greatest help.

I leave you in Allah's protection.

When I went home that day I threw out a rule I had always followed. I could not keep the day's proceedings to myself and told my family all that happened. They had only heard Afzal's name in the media, and did not know that we had been preparing for his hanging and I would be present at his execution. As I told them about Afzal's final hours, perhaps the only hanging that I really shared with them, we all cried together. I told them about my role, about the song he sang, and the note he left behind. This was the first time I broke down and cried.

I think about Afzal a lot and must have heard that song on YouTube endlessly. I know that anyone who refers to him is called an 'anti-national' but I think he was a good man who wanted to work with the NGO, People's Union of Civil Liberties. All he wanted was to serve humanity and for his people to live peacefully.

~

You see destiny playing out in strange ways in jail. Afzal Guru made a friend while at Tihar – Davinder Bhullar, the 1993 Delhi Blast convict, who was a Khalistan supporter, and sentenced to death three years before Afzal. They shared a great relationship, both being held in isolation as high security prisoners, and spent much of the little time they got walking together. Both were convicted and sentenced to death for terror attacks that killed people, and they both spent many years waiting for a decision on their mercy petition. But while Afzal was hanged, Davinder Bhullar's sentence was commuted in 2014. His lawyers successfully argued that the wait for a decision on his mercy petition had driven him to insanity. The Supreme Court agreed. In fact, by 2016, Bhullar had not only got a transfer to a Punjab jail, he also got parole from prison.

CRUSADER IN JAIL: ANNA HAZARE

The one continuous thread that runs through my three decades at Tihar is the story of money and muscle power in jail. The story plays out repeatedly with only the characters changing each time. I witnessed this first hand on my very first day at Tihar when Charles Sobhraj helped me secure the new job and ironically I saw it on the day I retired too, with many VIPs who were doing time in style. Some of us tried to change this to restore order and bring the guilty to book. But in the end, such crusaders had little or no success and the entrenched system always managed to win.

I experienced power being above the law in September 1986 when I was the deputy superintendent of the jail. Top industrialist, Lalit Mohan Thapar had been brought to Tihar because the Enforcement Directorate (ED) had found that his companies were involved in foreign exchange violations. He was the owner of several top notch companies including Crompton Greaves and lived in Delhi's most posh area of Amrita Shergill Marg. The dingy cell and the amenities that came with it were obviously not going to go down very well with Thapar.

On the very first day that Thapar was jailed, I got a call from Inspector General P.V. Sinhari at 4 am. His instruction was clear – I was to release Thapar immediately. I was shocked because it was blatantly against the rules to approach prisoners after lock-in unless there was an emergency. Furthermore, rules permitted release of prisoners only in the morning. The inspector general didn't push his point further and simply said that if those were the rules then I should go by them. But I knew this was not going to be the last I would hear about it. Sure enough, shortly after, somebody from the office of the then lieutenant governor of Delhi called me. I reiterated that I was bound by the rules and could not release Thapar at that hour. They informed me that a special bench of the Supreme Court headed by the Chief Justice of India had heard his bail petition at midnight and granted him relief.

'If Supreme Court has ordered his release then you can't detain him in jail,' the man on the line said. He was an aide at the LG's office but had all the airs of being the boss himself.

'The Supreme Court has done its work and given orders but jail rules are the Bible for us. We can't release him.'

They mounted further pressure, even reminded me of who wrote my 'Bible'.

'You know who wrote the rules? The LG. If he can write the jail rules, he can also change them.'

'But sir, you know that any change in rule does not work with retrospective effect. So even if you say that prisoners can from now forth be released in the middle of the night, it will not apply to L.M. Thapar.'

After many threats and cajoling which involved assuring me that if I were to release Thapar, I would not be held responsible, the aide from the LG's office gave up. I was adamant that I was not going to release Thapar. Why should I break the rules just because a rich person was in Tihar? A major factor behind my bravado was simply that I was in Delhi. If you are in the national capital, it is slightly more difficult for those in senior positions to pressurize you into doing things against your will. If I was in any other state, I would undoubtedly have been transferred. In this case, because I was part of a Delhi jail, all that they could have done was to transfer me from Jail number 1 to number 2 in Tihar itself. I also knew that if the press got a whiff of this story, it would draw a lot of flack for the LG's office. The media loves these kind of stories and the LG's office knew that if they escalated the issue, I would release the story of this undue interference.

The next day, as per the rules, I released L.M. Thapar just after 10 am. I remember that despite the kind of disturbance he had caused, Thapar was very graceful. He did not express any anger or irritation for having been detained in spite of obtaining bail from the top court. It was strange to see a gracious, polite man in contrast to the LG's minions who had threatened to change the laws just to help one individual. But if you are powerful or rich, people will do anything for you.

~

There were not too many officers in Tihar who inspired integrity. After P.V. Sinhari moved out as IG Prisons, many who came after him had a chequered record. I respected P.V. Sinhari for not pressurizing me to give in to the LG's office in releasing L.M. Thapar at an odd hour. There are not many who would have stood up to power like he did. This was not only because of a flaw in their personality but also the nature of the structure and hierarchy of the system. Earlier the rank of inspector general, was not specifically for prisons, but for a deputy commissioner of police with additional charge of prisons. That meant that IGs (now director general of prisons), were only half-interested in what happened at Tihar. They had far bigger fish to fry and this was only meant to be a kind of grimy waiting room, to be tolerated only until the train for a real job showed up. The IG's lack of skin-in-the-game explained why the superintendents of jails were god-like until then. Between the two posts, there is also a DIG of prisons. However, the real power lies with the superintendents because they are the boss of individual jails. They did all the wheeling, dealings and they hired and fired. Under the superintendent of the jail, there is the post of deputy superintendent (DS). There is DS (Grade 1) and junior to him is DS (Grade 2). Then comes the rank of the assistant superintendent followed by head warder. The lowest in the hierarchy were the warders of prisons. But it all changed post-1986 after the Charles Sobhraj jailbreak incident. The authorities then realized that Tihar needed a dedicated, full-time officer in charge and that is how a separate position was created. P.V. Sinhari was the first person to take charge of this position in May 1986.

I remember another incident with Sinhari quite vividly. During one of his rounds, he wanted to illustrate to a guard how to search a prisoner. He chose Karamvir Singh, a gangster who bit Sinhari's hand. Of course, he was punished by being put into solitary confinement for a while but it still tells you the kind of dangers that lurked if you became 'too active' in doing your duties. The gangster didn't forget either and kept sending threats to Sinhari. The officer responded by keeping a loaded revolver at his desk all the time.

When Sinhari left in June 1988, he was succeeded by a Bengal cadre officer, H.P. Kumar. The prison system hierarchy is led by the title of DGP, his deputy is called additional inspector general (IG). The IG has two DIGs (Prisons) reporting to him/her, who have 18 SPs and then the DS of both grades, followed by ASP and warders.

All the good that Sinhari had done in Tihar with his temperament, Kumar, it is safe to say, undid. If Sinhari challenged gangsters in jail, Kumar was more timid. He knew he had to spend only a few years at Tihar and was therefore disinterested in doing any real work. He never took rounds, spent only a few hours in his office and preferred to spend more time engaged in spiritual activities. We remember H.P. Kumar as the man who would be chanting *'Ram, Ram, Ram'* incessantly. Unfortunately, the good Lord couldn't help him and under his watch Tihar reverted to being the gangster den it was before Sinhari. There was no longer a confrontation between the good officers and the gangsters. The latter had a free run.

It is a commonly held view that the post of IG Prisons is a punishment posting. It was usually reserved for those who were either an irritant to the Delhi commissioner of police, or someone who posed a threat to them. It was true of R.K. Sharma, who is not to be confused with the top cop charged with the murder of journalist Shivani Bhatnagar. He was a UT cadre officer as listless in his job as his predecessor Kumar, without any motivation to bring about jail reform. They would spend their time handling queries from Parliament or from courts. Most of those too, they palmed them off to me. I didn't mind because I had a good rapport with all of the bosses and preferred this work to handling jail administration. But that too, changed in 1993.

As R.K. Sharma left for another posting, there was talk of the first woman to join the IPS, Kiran Bedi, coming to Tihar to be our new boss. Never before in the history of Tihar did a transfer create so much enthusiasm. Kiran Bedi was known to be a rebel and she was being sent to Tihar for a 'punishment posting' as well. The most famous story about her was how she had taken action even against Prime Minister Indira Gandhi's car for a traffic violation. She was a darling of the media. Until now we were headed by officers who at best were biding their time waiting for a better posting, in other words no one very inspirational. Kiran Bedi was a cop with multiple degrees in law, political science and social science. She had already established herself as an activist with her non-governmental organization called Navjyoti that was meant to promote crime prevention by working with the community, imparting skills to street children and detox programmes. So, while all the IGs before her were anonymous officers who you only got to know once you started working with them, Kiran Bedi's reputation was known across the country. And in 1993, she became our boss at the age of 44.

You could say that we were all in awe of her. She brought with her hope – a woman who had built her reputation by not being intimidated by even the prime minister of the country. Surely, this was the kind of iron will, we needed to set things in order at Tihar. 'Sunilji, I think good days are here for you,' many of my friends told me. I was not sure what they meant. Maybe they meant to be sarcastic because they knew I was a stickler for rules but I was genuinely excited to have someone who believed in reform, becoming our supervisor.

On her first day at Tihar, Kiran Bedi called a meeting of all the superintendents and the deputy superintendents. This was unusual because generally people liked to take a few days to get things going. She passed around sheets of paper to everyone and urged us to write down suggestions for improvement. 'If you don't want to say out loud what we need to do to fix things,' she said, 'Just write it down.' We all did as we were asked. These weekly meetings were a key part of her way of functioning.

Outside Tihar, she was known as the tough, lathi-wielding cop literally using the stick to bring the errant system in line, but we witnessed a different side to her. It was one which employed interesting techniques to get us to toe the line. For instance, the weekly meetings she instituted were conducted over lunch where we were all encouraged to bring our own food and share with others. She would also chip in – sometimes she would bring sweetmeats like *kheer* or *halwa* and would serve everyone personally. She was especially considerate and kind to the junior staff.

Her objective was to make everyone comfortable so they would discuss their problems and challenges openly. During regular working hours, she initiated an open office system where she never closed her door to anyone. There were special instructions issued that anyone from the staff or even the public should be allowed to see her, if they wished. She kept a writing pad with her and would record everything people discussed with her. Her approach had a significant impact on the collective morale of the jail staff. Of course, it went much beyond matters related to Tihar. Due to her fame, many regular people would come to meet her looking for favours

– assistance in their child's admission to school, help with a job or clearing loans. The thing about Kiran Bedi was that she listened to them all. She did not so much go by the rules but just listened with her heart. She also thrived on all the adulation she got. The public meetings became a part of the daily routine where everyone participated. Sometimes, people would bring up legal issues too, such as if their family members were wrongfully imprisoned. When she felt they were genuine, she would fight for them. All those who had been harassed by prison officials, or had been denied meetings with relatives, now had an effective redressal system to turn to.

Let me tell you about one such instance that took place just a fortnight after she joined Tihar. A notorious prisoner of Jail number 4, Sardara, was a drug dealer and one of the worst kinds of men we had to deal with. As a result, he received a beating at the hands of the prison officials because of his regular unruly behaviour. Kiran Bedi was furious that this had happened under her watch and wanted to know who was behind the abuse of authority. We were concerned because unlike other IGs who would have ordered an inquiry, but turned a blind eye to the consequences, Kiran Bedi was not going to let us off so easily. What she did next shocked us all – at lunch time, she announced that she would not eat until someone took responsibility for the beating. They would have to own up, apologize and commit to never assaulting a prisoner again. She had adopted Gandhi's means of *satyagraha* in perhaps the most violent jail in India!

A day went by, and another. Her deputy, Inspector General Jaidev Sarangi, informed us that she was adamant on not communicating with us until someone owned up. When we met her, she told us, 'When I've given clear instructions that no one is to be beaten, why did you do it?' Seeing that she was not about to give in, I gathered courage and finally spoke up, 'Madam, he was a very unruly prisoner.' This explanation did not move her – she wanted us to promise that we would never repeat this again. So after three days, all of us apologized to her. She had zero tolerance for violence against prisoners, no matter how 'justifiable' it was. Her method of not speaking to those who flouted this rule was not a one off, but her chosen mode of implementing the rules. When we complained that non-violence made us look soft and fuzzy as opposed to tough jailers, she retorted, 'It's not like you hit gangsters. You hit only those people who are vulnerable, the ones you can extort money from. You don't have the guts to hit gangsters, a serial killer, or a terrorist, only the poor. So, if you have come here to talk about discipline, it's all a lie.' She was right.

That was not the end of it, though. Soon an order was issued which transferred me from my comfortable position of legal officer back to the grind of being the deputy superintendent of Sardara's jail, i.e. Jail number 4. I was furious with her. I had been in this position for 12 years by then and no DG or IG had removed me. My work required precision and knowledge of the law and I took pride in the fact that I could do it well, keeping in mind the sensitivities of all involved. Tihar had always been involved in tricky legal fights and I had managed to extract them from many scandals. And now suddenly, my boss had decided that I was dispensable? I felt humiliated by what I saw as a demotion and because of this I began resenting her. I didn't bother telling her about it or how much it upset me.

This was 1993 and I had no choice but to accept the challenge because it would go on my record if I refused the new post. Why was it a challenge? Because Jail number 4 had people like Jaswinder Singh alias Jassa, who considered himself to be the real boss of Tihar. He would flaunt the numerous murder cases against him and took pride in his gangster cred. Originally from Delhi, he had committed so many murders that punishment for another was not a deterrent for him and so everyone, including me, was fearful of him. Actually fearful was an understatement. The judge in Jassa's case was so terrified about his safety, he refused to give any order in the case. He simply recused himself. And he wasn't the only judge to do so. Jassa would openly threaten us all – I had two clear choices, either be scared of him or to make him toe the line.

In reality, all I had to do was to enforce the already laid down rules of Tihar – any one of them which would hit Jassa hard. I chose to threaten him by taking away the favouritism he enjoyed in the allotment of cells. Self-styled gangsters in Tihar exercised power by marking out areas or empires for themselves inside the prison. It's a system that still exists. Each strong man identifies a particular cell/barrack that becomes their territory, and get other members of their entourage to be moved there. The entourage and other followers pay protection money or do tasks for the leader and in return, they get protection and basic necessities like food, mobile phones, meetings from him. The regular food that is served in Tihar is less than optimum, so the leader uses his influence to have it supplemented with extras from the canteen and in some cases even gets a flunky to cook. A cosy ecosystem thrived in different parts of the jail with our own officials sitting on top like parasites. People like Jassa either intimidated them into looking the other way or more likely, bribed them into doing so. The ones that did not benefit from it were too scared to speak up and so turned a blind eye.

This arrangement enabled Jassa's behaviour – he had two cells to himself. One was dedicated solely to him and he lived there comfortably, while the second cell adjacent to his was where he kept pigeons as pets. In a jail that has always been overcrowded, Jassa had enough space to keep pets! A 2015 report of the National Crime Records Bureau found that Tihar was overcrowded by 226 per cent, with some prisoners sleeping in sitting position because there was simply no room for them to stretch and lie down. About 10 out of 30 cells in that particular jail housed Jassa's cronies. My predecessor apparently had an understanding with him that whenever a new prisoner entered Tihar, especially if they were rich, they would be sent to Jassa's care. He would then decide what kind of incarceration to give him – a comfortable living situation or a nightmarish one. It was Jassa who decided who would receive solitary treatment. It was as if there was a jail within Tihar and Jassa was the jailer.

The first order I issued after taking over Jail number 4, was to allocate accommodation according to alphabetical order. It may not sound too radical but it meant that Jassa would be moved and so would his hangers-on from the empire that he had nurtured. I was disrupting the system that he had set up, and this meant he would stop getting protection money from the cronies who he helped get a berth in his barrack. I was asserting control over his turf.

It was all very well to pass such an order but who was going to implement it? My team flatly refused, saying they had children and feared for their safety. That was the wondrous thing about Tihar. So what if I was the boss, I could not force my staff to do anything. So I decided I would remove Jassa myself. I still remember the scene that greeted me as I reached his ward. The word had already reached him that I was coming to remove him from his cell. When I reached his cell with a handful of constables, who had no option but to tag along, I saw Jassa and one of his close associates, Chandrashekhar, standing and smoking (smoking had not yet been banned and we used to sell tobacco and cigarettes in the jail canteen).

The scene was akin to a Western movie, where both of us sized each other up.

'What's the matter?' I asked

'Why don't you switch the alarm on?' said Jassa, challenging me. The alarm was a signal of emergency and would have indicated a full-on jail riot. My constables stood on the sidelines, waiting to witness me getting beaten up.

'If I had to put the alarm on, Jassa, why would I come to meet you?'

I made a decision very quickly – there was not much point in escalating things with Jassa at this point. The constables, supposedly here to back me up, were not entirely on my side. I had the feeling that they were more here to watch the drama unfold and then report the sordid details to everyone. Even if Jassa were to curse me once, the story would be exaggerated manifold and word would spread of my assault and how I was taught a lesson by the brutes of Tihar. I was not about to give this kind of satisfaction to my colleagues. So I took a more conciliatory tone and asked Jassa if we could step inside his cell to talk.

'Why aren't you following my order about the new ward allocation?' I asked.

'Why are you undermining me by moving us? I have respect here, everybody knows us. If you want to get me killed, well, then we will see who gets killed.'

That was a veiled threat if ever there was one. Just then, someone shouted that Jassa had a knife which could hurt me.

'Hand it over,' I said.

'They're just talking nonsense.'

After some back and forth and cajoling on my part, Jassa finally brought out the knife, which was more like a two-and-a-half-foot-long sword. 'They told me to use this on you to sort it out,' he said. And by they, he obviously meant my colleagues. Apparently, they did not like my attitude which they thought to be pretentious and superior. By this point I was very stressed as I realized how unsafe the situation was for me and decided to rework my entire strategy. I negotiated with him, 'Hand over the knife, and I will let you be. But the hangers-on have to go.' Jassa did not want to agree to this but I thought it could wait another day. I knew that hardened criminals like Jassa did not stop at anything if they did not get their way. If you disrupted the carefully constructed jail routine they had made for themselves, they could kill you, even if you were jail authority. That's the reason the wise just stayed away and let the convict or *numberdar* administrators sort it out using their primitive, jungle law ways.

I related the entire incident to Kiran Bedi. She called yet another meeting and sacked prison officials, who it was determined, were helping Jassa. I was now going to be the sole deputy superintendent in-charge of Jail number 4 – she had given me more responsibility. The long-term impact of the Jassa drama was the steps we put in place to separate hardened criminals like him from those who they could harm or exploit. At that time, I let him stay but Kiran Bedi created a high security ward where we started housing the real terrors of Tihar. They were profiled, identified and kept under the extra security of the Tamil Nadu Police forces and entirely isolated from the rest of the prisoners. Having no pool of vulnerable new inmates to harass, these prisoners took us to court in 1994. They were all inmates of Jail number 1 (where HSW [High-Security Ward] was created), including Jassa. But, we won this battle and followed our success with another initiative. This time we separated first-time offenders or young ones in a dedicated place. It has been documented in various studies that even if you are not a criminal, you become one if you spend time in jail. So, we created a kind of 'safe zone' for those who were only there for less than six months. Most of them would get released in the first week itself and our new system isolated them from exploitation. While this did not solve the problem of harassment for good, it did provide at least one layer of safety net. With 15-20 such criminals from my jail being shifted to the high-security ward, my job became much easier for a while. I was lucky because Jassa also eventually resigned to being in the high-security ward. I plied his cell with several religious books – the Gita and the Vedas. I'm told he liked reading this and whether it is connected or not, he decided not to revolt against the shifting after that. This was a major relief because if Jassa wasn't rebelling, neither was anyone else in the high-security ward.

Ms. Bedi was transferred from Tihar after two years in 1995 (see chapter 2 for why this happened). During her time at Tihar, she introduced many reforms that had a lasting impact on the jail. She publicized a programme through which volunteers from various professions could come and share their expertise with prisoners. Doctors, educators, social workers – she invited them all to become shareholders in the community reform process. She even reimbursed them Rs 50 for their commute to jail. This initiative saw tremendous response. Many doctors, teachers and schools joined in with societies donating stationery for inmates. The only reason why I believe it became so popular is because of Kiran Bedi's personality. The other initiatives included introducing vipassana and meditation to the prisoners. In 1975, vipassana was tried at the Jaipur Central jail and while it got great feedback, no one had the vision to take it to jails in other parts of the country. In November 1993, we started with our first class, which was held by Guru S.N. Goenka and 200 other teachers and have never looked back since. This programme was historic as it was attended by 1100 inmates from Delhi jails. For some like the 'Tandoor case' murderer Sushil Sharma, who served 23 years in Tihar and is now free, vipassana was a lifesaver, a source of hope, a coping strategy when everything appeared bleak.

Suddenly we were being written about in both the national and international media. In fact, for the first time, Tihar started getting good press. Kiran Bedi was awarded the prestigious Magsaysay award in 1994. Her reform work in prison impressed Mother Teresa who expressed a wish to meet her. A year later, in 1995, President Bill Clinton invited her to a breakfast prayer meeting with Mother Teresa. The buzz about Tihar Jail had become truly global, with England inviting her to examine their prison system. In her short two years, Tihar's image changed but it did not last long.

~

Kiran Bedi and I kept in touch and I would see her now and then but her proper homecoming to Tihar came sixteen years later. In August 2011, Kiran Bedi visited Tihar as a full-time anti-corruption crusader. No longer held back by the trappings of her police uniform, she was now a part of Team Anna, a group of civil society activists that had come together to demand a tough legislation to counter corruption. Their leader was 74-year-old former army soldier Anna Hazare, who was slight in frame but had taken the entire country by storm by demanding a law that would probe everyone from the prime minister to senior judges. The idea terrified those in power. It was a movement that fired up all our imaginations and even government officials like me secretly backed him.

Anna Hazare landed in Delhi from his native village of Ralegan Siddhi in Maharashtra, and made the then UPA government very nervous. He was to sit on dharna at Delhi's JP Park in Ferozeshah Kotla against the recent corruption scams such as the telecom scam, which certain government ministers were involved in. The public mood was angry and the government feared that Hazare's dharna could turn into a call to overthrow them. They decided to put Anna Hazare and his associate, another Magsaysay award winner, Arvind Kejriwal into preventive arrest. Along with them were other key people like Sri Sri Ravi Shankar's Art of Living Team member, Maheish Girri. Girri and Bedi would go on to become bonafide members of the Bharatiya Janata Party with Girri as an MP from Delhi and Bedi moving to Puducherry as governor, after losing the Delhi polls in 2015. But much before that, they were all under the umbrella group 'India Against Corruption'. They claimed to be apolitical and had a diverse list of members although one common ground was that they were all opposed to the UPA government's policies.

By arresting them, the government thought they could contain their followers and keep them off the streets from protesting. It turned out to be a complete miscalculation. From the time that Anna Hazare was brought to Tihar at 4 pm on 16 August, crowds began to gather outside the jail. About 1,500 protestors who had accompanied Anna were also taken into detention. We had no space for them so the then Lieutenant Governor Tejendra Khanna ordered Chhatrasal Stadium and a stadium in Bawana to be converted into a special jail.

But it was a PR disaster and the government had to backtrack as quickly as possible. The rumblings of dissent grew louder as word spread of a frail man being dragged to jail by the might of a government because they were afraid of the consequences of his non-violent agitation. From outside the environs of our prison in West Delhi to Parliament House, there were protests everywhere. The opposition party, BJP, ridiculed the government and asked why it was afraid of Anna Hazare. His supporters chanted '*Anna Hazare Zindabad*' and '*Bharat Mata ki Jai*' as the numbers kept swelling. The government soon ordered Anna's release and withdrew the case.

Anna, Kejriwal and their colleagues were all lodged in Jail number 4, which was an interesting coincidence. The people they had protested against as symbols of corruption, from Telecom Minister A. Raja, who was accused in the 2G Spectrum Scam to Congress leader Suresh Kalmadi, accused in the Commonwealth Games scam, were all residents of the same jail. They were all in the same vicinity, close enough for them to come face to face with each other. But, we wanted to avoid such an interaction (much to the media's dismay!). Journalists would call me to ask if the men accused in the 2G Spectrum scam and Team Anna had met. We emptied out an entire barrack for Anna Hazare, but soon after, we were informed that we had to release him.

'We won't leave.' These words were voiced by former bureaucrat Arvind Kejriwal, who had figured out the government's plan. Suddenly we had a new problem. 'We won't leave jail until the government gives in to our demand and lets us protest.' We tried to reason with them that Tihar had nothing to do with this fight, and that we could not decide on their demand to protest. When they were sent to judicial custody, we took them in. Now that the case was dropped, we wanted them to leave. But Team Anna was in no mood to budge. That is when the games started.

Deputy superintendent of the jail, Shivraj Yadav (the same one who was punished for Charles Sobhraj's escape), came up with a plan. He told Team Anna that the government had sent representatives to discuss their demands but if they wanted to negotiate they would have to leave their cells and come to the jail headquarters. The idea being that once they left Jail number 4, they were out of custody. The superintendent, along with Yadav, accompanied them to the headquarters where my office was. They were taken to the director general's office to wait for the negotiating team.

Outside, Team Anna's supporters had become unmanageable. They were young and very aggressive and had surrounded our jail compound from every direction. It was getting tough to even leave home because of them. We knew we had to get Anna and Kejriwal out of Tihar soon. Technically, since we had managed to get them out of Jail number 4, Neeraj Kumar, the then director general at the time, asked me to immediately give a statement to the media that they had been released from jail. He felt this would calm down Anna's angry followers.

I did what I was told and went to the entry gate of both Jail number 1 and 3. I informed a bunch of journalists waiting outside gate number 3 that Anna Hazare had been released. I did not know it then but this became an iconic clipping and in days to come this statement of mine would run repeatedly on TV. After I gave the statement, I came back to the headquarters to find it teeming with policemen of all ranks – SHOs, ACPs, DCPs. We all started speculating – is the government planning to ambush these activists and drag them out of jail? Just a couple of months before, another anti-corruption champion, yoga evangelist Baba Ramdev's dharna was interrupted in the middle of the night by police officers who picked him up and flew him out of Delhi. The police action was ugly and led to one person being killed too. It became a major embarrassment for the UPA government because top ministers had tried to defuse the situation and when there was a death, they were blamed for it too. It became a turning point in the UPA's downward slide and they could not afford a repeat of that situation. Were we going to see this old man being dragged to Ralegaon Siddhi?

I was lost in these thoughts when the man in question called out to me. '*Arrey*! How can you say on TV that I have been released from jail?'

I smiled meekly. 'Anna ji, we have released you from jail. You are in the jail headquarters, which is almost 2 kilometres away.'

'Really? We have been released from jail? But the deputy superintendent brought us here promising that somebody from the government will speak to us. Were you cheating us? This is very bad. I know that when you are released from jail, your thumb impression is taken. That has not happened and I will not allow it. I don't want to get released from jail until our demands are met. We will sit here in this very room and be on dharna. You do whatever you have to, rain bullets on us, anything you want, we won't budge.'

I was in trouble. The nation's darling and anti-corruption's poster boy had seen me on TV making what he saw as a 'false statement' and it was in fact, a bit misleading. I approached Arvind Kejriwal for help because we needed to get them out of our office. 'Why are you doing this? Is your agitation against us? Why are you disturbing our work?' I asked him. 'Everyone says he only listens to you, so please explain to him that you have to leave this place.' By then the media had also figured out there was something wrong. I had told them on record that Anna and his colleagues were free to go but there was no sign of them leaving Tihar.

'*Kasam se* (I swear),' Arvind Kejriwal said to me, 'He doesn't listen to me. Anna does what he thinks is right.'

It was going to be a long night for all of us. We requested them to move from the DG's office to the conference room which was air-conditioned, and provided them clean bedsheets to use. The room also had an attached bathroom for their use. Anna and 12 others spent the night in this room while hundreds of their supporters slept on the roads surrounding Tihar. By now public support was so strong that all roads around Tihar were shut down.

The next morning, on 17 August the reality that we had a senior citizen who had insisted on going on a fast dawned on us. Arvind Kejriwal, being a diabetic, was not fasting as his doctors had advised against it, but the others were refusing to eat. Meanwhile their supporters on the streets kept the pressure on. They were very organized – no one went hungry as the volunteers cooked on the pavements and handed out food parcels to all those who had camped outside Tihar. It was nothing like we had seen before.

We kept cajoling Anna that he should leave jail but he was very shrewd. He realized he had the government just where he wanted them – under his thumb. 'Do you think if I leave from here, they will care about me or my demands? No, I am not going.' As he continued his fast, his health deteriorated but he refused to get himself examined by the Tihar designated doctor from GB Pant Hospital. Finally, Anna said he would only agree to a check-up by his own doctor, the famous Dr. Naresh Trehan. We had no choice but to agree. However, this was easier said than done.

Dr. Trehan agreed to come immediately and brought along an ambulance with him. As soon as the crowds outside Tihar saw the ambulance, they surrounded it. They thought the government had begun aggressive action to remove Anna Hazare from jail. I was tasked with getting Dr. Trehan inside to see Anna, and tried to convince the crowd outside to let us through. After much chaos in Delhi's muggy August weather, we finally sneaked Dr. Trehan in through the back exit. Fortunately, Anna was not too difficult and allowed Dr. Trehan to do the check-up. If I recall correctly, Dr. Trehan had treated him earlier for high blood pressure and a related heart condition and the two knew each other well. They spent quite some time talking fondly to each other.

A whole host of interesting personalities like Nana Patekar, Swami Agnivesh and Sri Sri Ravi Shankar came to visit Anna. Dr Kiran Bedi, by then a vocal critic of the government and the establishment, asked to come see Anna which got us into further trouble. When she came to meet him she also recorded a message from Anna on her phone. In the 10-odd minute clip which went viral almost instantly, a cheerful Anna Hazare is heard telling his supporters how he is reinvigorated due to the support of all the young people. 'I was feeling tired but I now feel I can continue for days,' he said. Kiran Bedi kept asking him questions and the short interview enraged the government even further.

Team Anna's PR machinery was so efficient they found ways to continue feeding the supporters and media with bits of information. When they were not making videos, Kejriwal's aide and future Delhi deputy chief minister, Manish Sisodia would address the people on the streets from time to time. Arvind Kejriwal would also step aside to shout '*Bharat Mata ki jai*' – there was absolutely no restriction on his movement at all. But, after two-three days, all this got too much. Neeraj Kumar was hopping mad. Not only was he trying to control the situation inside Tihar, he suddenly had a volley of visitors to deal with, as whoever came to meet Anna would also drop in to see him.

Neeraj Kumar had been on leave when Anna and his supporters had first been sent to Tihar, but he returned on 18 August and realized this situation could not continue as is. I also think he had been hauled up by the then Home Minister P. Chidambaram. It is only when faced with this kind of pressure that the bosses get angry and want to pin the blame on someone. He told us off for our poor handling of the situation and said that we had failed in our duty in not getting Team Anna out of jail. We could tell he was feeling the pressure from 'upstairs' – why else would the Delhi Police be sitting in our office, waiting for further instructions from the Ministry of Home Affairs. These instructions never came because Chidambaram told them to not aggravate the situation any further but just to stabilize it. But the anti-government slogans streaming in from our windows were certainly not helping Neeraj Kumar's mood.

DIG R.N. Sharma and I explained to him that the root of the trouble was Arvind Kejriwal. We told him Anna Hazare did not want to protest in the jail premises, but Kejriwal had convinced him otherwise. An angry and determined Neeraj Kumar said, 'Call him.' When Arvind Kejriwal came, Neeraj Kumar thundered, 'Why are you doing this? Why are you instigating Anna Hazare ji to protest here in jail? You have a problem with the government, speak to the government! Why are you obstructing our work?'

And Kejriwal said the same thing he said to me that first night. 'I assure you, I didn't say anything to him. He does as he pleases.'

'Speak to Anna Hazare and tell him he shouldn't obstruct our work, please vacate the premises.'

'Yes, I will try.'

On 19 August, when Anna and gang finally left Tihar it was not because Neeraj Kumar and all of us had effective persuasion skills, but because they had finally got what they wanted. The Delhi Police gave them permission to continue their agitation at Ramlila Maidan. It was a victory for them.

The next day, in anticipation of their move, all our exits were sealed. A major concern was that in their enthusiasm to greet Anna Hazare, his supporters would damage our premises. All court appearances of other prisoners that day were cancelled and we eyed the hundreds of people gathered outside with some trepidation. TV channels had been building up a crescendo since the previous night and the situation looked fragile. When we accompanied them out, hundreds of people gathered moved towards us and a makeshift stage was created. Anna Hazare had once again got the mighty government to bend and he was about to share this moment of glory with his people. Standing there listening to him, I was quite impressed because unlike many other VIPs who exaggerate everything inside jail, he only spoke the truth. And the crowds listened. As they moved towards Ramlila Maidan, they gathered on rooftops, on trucks, to just catch a glimpse of him and his associates – the anti-corruption crusaders promising to fix the corruption that had afflicted each aspect of daily life in our country. Who could identify with that more than us who worked in Tihar?

THE DESPERATE WORLD OF TIHAR

In the monsoon of 2002, there were signs of a major upheaval in police circles. Delhi Police was finally about to arrest one of their own – a powerful officer accused of conspiring to murder journalist Shivani Bhatnagar. The crime was committed on 23 January 1999, when the body of the Indian Express journalist was found just a few feet away from her crying baby, at her home in IP Extension of Patparganj, across the river Yamuna. Bhatnagar was an investigative journalist and was considered close to IPS officer R.K. Sharma who was posted in the Prime Minister's Office (PMO) at that time. The police's case was that Bhatnagar was working on a story that was not favourable to Sharma, which is why he planned her murder and hired hitmen to carry out the killing. When they framed charges, they also spoke about the 'physical intimacy' between Bhatnagar and Sharma which they claimed threatened to 'spoil his life and his career'.

The Shivani Bhatnagar story has a long history. For three and a half years, there was no lead in the case and then suddenly, the first arrest was made on 30 July 2002. A breakthrough had finally come. As soon as this breakthrough happened, R.K. Sharma went on leave knowing that he was going to be next. At the time he was Inspector General (IG) Prisons in Haryana, making him the top boss of prisons in the state. Due to his incredible networking skills, he had held other important positions in the past. Apart from the posting at the PMO, he had also served in the CBI, who had sent him on a posting to Interpol in Lyon, France. While there, he had done exceedingly well and had even learnt to speak French. He was arguably one of the most famous police officers in the country at the time. And yet from 1 August, when a non-bailable warrant was issued against him, he was reported to be untraceable by the police.

It was one of the most mysterious, unsuccessful manhunts launched by the police because Sharma managed to evade arrest for almost two months. It's an open secret in security circles that if the police really want to, they can trace anyone. But this was not just anybody, Sharma was one of their own, so the inability to find him was especially suspicious to many. On 27 September, two months after the first arrest, Sharma finally decided to surrender. By then apparently, his property papers were all settled so that the investigators could not touch it at all as 'proceeds of crime' even if they wanted to. What I got to know later from the staff of Ambala prisons was that R.K. Sharma was rumoured to be hiding out in Ambala jail all this time! So while the police had suspected that Sharma had run away from Delhi, he had actually been enjoying the government's hospitality and that too right under the nose of security personnel who were aware of the hunt for him. Clearly however, their conscience did not force them to give him up.

This may give you an idea of just how entrenched corruption is in our system. I would like to tell you there was poetic justice as the inspector general of prisons did time in Tihar, but that would be misleading. In the nine years that Sharma spent in Tihar, he continued to wield tremendous power and the police swagger did not leave him, despite the fact that he had been stripped off his police medal. In fact, he would speak to all of us as if we were his subordinates. When it came to R.K. Sharma, jail rules were either flaunted or totally ignored. His family did not have to seek a formal appointment for a *mulaqat* and throughout his time behind bars, influential Haryana police officers continued to visit Sharma. His wife would drop in to meet the boss Ajay Aggarwal frequently and then meet her husband in the deputy superintendent's room. It was as if murdering a woman was a petty crime. Or maybe, the status of the perpetrator always comes before his crime.

~

I would like to claim that by the time I left Tihar it was cleaner and less corrupt than when I had joined. That after 35 years, the jungle raj I had encountered in 1981 was now civilized and that there were measures in place to stop the blatant disregard for prison rules. But I would be lying if I said this. The truth is that things remained the same. My colleagues, save a few notable exceptions, were abettors who when faced with someone unwilling to join them in their misconduct, would try to find ways to negate their work. I watched their modes of operation with both fascination and disgust.

There was one jailer who used his anger to do this effectively. He deliberately cultivated a reputation of losing his temper suddenly and beating up whoever was around. He also picked on those prisoners who had the ability to pay. The way to do this was by the very careful profiling that was done in the *mulaiza* (ward) for a new entrant. If they seemed to know the director general of the prison or other senior officials, then you marked them out to be people who were not to be messed with. But all other inmates of comfortable means were fair game. This particular officer, known to have a fiery temper, would beat them for no reason. Prisoners would be terrorized by the sight of him and would be advised to ingratiate themselves to the 'angry officer' with gifts, or else the beatings would continue. Mission accomplished. The angry officer was so particular about his image he would also scold and threaten other jail staff if they extorted someone and did not share the proceeds with him. This created a convenient ecosystem where they all jointly collected bribes and lived off it.

However, for some money was not the only impetus. Caste too, played an important role in jail. One of my colleagues, a deputy superintendent, fashioned himself to be a Jat leader. Any inmate or staffer, who was a Jat, was under his protection, and his motto was that a Jat never kneels in front of anyone. It sounds dramatic but actually he was quite bold. Whenever someone was being too much of a troublemaker, I would ask him to take care of the matter. He would teach the prisoner a lesson which was quite useful. When I say a lesson, it meant that he got convicts to beat him up. Having said this, I'll admit that he was corrupt as well. All the protection that he gave Jat inmates came for a price. As soon as they would come to Tihar, he would send out a message to their families that he was the one to contact if they needed anything. I can tell you that he lived quite comfortably.

So what services can you buy from the 'angry officer' or the Jat officer? If you are millionaires like real estate giant Unitech's Ajay and Sanjay Chandra, then you can arrange for an entire household's worth of comforts to make your stay in jail bearable. The Chandras were sent to jail in March 2017 because they cheated 16,000 home-buyers of their money. The Supreme Court refused to give them bail until they provided a sum of Rs 750 crores in lieu of the homes that they had failed to hand over to the home-buyers and the money they had bungled out of the escrow.

In court, the Chandras claimed Unitech was in a dire financial state because of the 2008 financial crisis and therefore they could not afford to hand over the homes as promised. That and being implicated in the spectrum allocation scandal ensured that they had to spend time in jail, but it was clear that these wealthy men had no intention of living the austere life that was required of an ordinary prisoner. As per the rules, they would only be able to meet their families twice a week for 30 minutes, would have to eat the food prepared in jail and sleep on the floor or cement 'beds'. In addition, their movement would be curtailed inside the ward or their barrack.

But none of these rules seemed to apply to the Chandras. After other prisoners complained, an inquiry was conducted in Tihar, which revealed that they moved around the jail freely, had access to smartphones, coolers, food from home twice a day and meetings with family even on weekends. While ordinary prisoners had holes in the ground overflowing with excreta, they had western-style toilets. When their families were not visiting, they had a 32-inch LED TV, coconut water along with bottled water and thick mattresses to cool their heels. The fans in the other prisoners' barracks are hardly effective in Delhi's cruel summer because they are protected by a thick wire mesh. In the Chandra brothers' cell, the fans were, however, freed from the mesh. Their cell had been protected from the jealous eyes of other inmates by blankets, and in doing so they also had the most prized possession in prison – privacy. They were given space to work, equipped with computers and internet connections and that too just opposite the superintendent of jail's office. Ramesh Kumar, the visiting judge who had conducted the inquiry and made the report, concluded that the director general of prisons should face a criminal case for what was an obvious case of corruption.

This report was published in 2016. I had already retired by then, but it did not surprise me at all. None of their crimes were original. While creating an entire office inside Tihar was certainly audacious, the use of cell phones was the oldest trick in the book. We have strict inspections, including cavity searches, to detect for contraband items such as phones. Therefore, it is impossible for an inmate or their visitor to smuggle it in – a cell phone inside prison can only be given to you by a jail official.

This is what my encounter with drug lord Sharafat Sheikh taught me. Sometime in 2010 (I remember that it was a Sunday), the director general at the time, B.K. Gupta, summoned me and said that the crime branch wanted to raid our high-security ward because they were certain that someone was using a phone inside. The idea of a phone inside the high-security ward sounded ridiculous because you would think that there would be extra security to prevent this. And yet, it made perfect sense too. If you managed to procure a phone with help from friends that were jail authorities, you could easily use it because no other prisoner would be there to rat on you. B.K. Gupta's brief to me was to help the police team extract that phone with minimum fuss.

So, off we went and Sharafat Sheikh, true to his name, was politeness personified.

'Guptaji, I've heard such good things about you. Ayub Khan Saheb praises you a lot.' Flattery was one way to go, I suppose.

'We have to search your cell.'

Sharafat Sheikh objected. He said that he did not want his cell, which had the Holy Quran, desecrated. 'It will be better if you don't go inside,' he said.

We would not back down and when he saw that he was not going to get his way, he asked us to remove our shoes. We refused. Instead, I suggested he bring the holy book out of his cell. He finally agreed. The Tamil Nadu police team and I went in and found not one, but two phones hidden in the toilet seat. The police team was pleased because they claimed they got sensitive information about a drug racket from those phones. They registered a case against Sharafat Sheikh for the possession of phones inside prison.

Before I left, Sheikh said to me, 'Guptaji, you have cost me 50,000 rupees. Mobile phones have gone, that's not an issue, I will get another by this evening.' He said, pausing for impact. 'There are many who get me the phones because I cannot live without it. It's a matter of survival for me.'

He was not exaggerating. Two weeks later, we raided his cell again and found another mobile phone. The rumour was that a senior officer had passed on the phone to him. After all, who would check the boss!

On another occasion we received a complaint against a high-profile prisoner, the arms dealer Abhishek Verma, who was in prison because he was accused of leaking official secrets. He was supposedly allowed a satellite phone by the jail superintendent himself. But, we could never prove this. When we checked his cell we found pen-drives and objectionable photos of women instead. The son of Congress leader Srikant Verma, Abhishek was a flamboyant businessman who loved the good life. He did not adhere to the rule of only having five sets of shirts and pants to wear in prison. For court hearings, he would show up in designer clothes by expensive brands such as Hermes.

Jail rules are not universal. While the rich and powerful have satellite and mobile phones, the poor have to live with lack of medication and clean water. Soft mattresses for the privileged, but lack of sleeping space for others. No utensils for regular inmates, while cooking meals is the norm for some. So what do people like me do?

The decision not to participate in the rampant corruption often led to trouble for me. One form of this was relatively harmless, just mental harassment. For example, somewhere in 1991 or 1992, I saw my subordinate, Assistant Superintendent B.S. Negi accepting cash from somebody. I instantly told him off and shamed him for selling out despite being an officer. His way of seeking revenge was to show me how close he was to a politician staying in jail at the time. Madan Bhaiya was a member of the UP legislature at the time and was serving time in jail in 1991–92 for a kidnapping case. In an attempt to intimidate me, Negi would spend a lot of time with Madan Bhaiya. When I asked him why, he would respond nonchalantly, 'I was just having tea.' He would get Madan Bhaiya to insult me and put me down in whatever way he could. He was a politician and so even in jail, he had power over all of us. Incidentally, Negi and his son organized an attack on me and after I filed a criminal case, they were arrested in 1995.

The other mode of harassment was more dangerous. Influential inmates would file complaints against officers like me and leak it to newspapers. The complaints were filed with the support of jail staff but had imaginative grounds. For instance, one said that I was smuggling smack into jail. I was stunned not so much by the fact that someone had complained against me, but by the absurd nature of it. They were calling me a drug dealer now? Then, it struck me that maybe they were just projecting a practice they themselves were involved in. Deflection, after all, is a common trick. The complainant, Surender Grover, was a prisoner facing a murder trial who fancied himself to be a 'human rights activist'. He was educated and fluent in English and would encourage others to bring their problems to him.

I had to get to the bottom of the accusation he had levelled against me. So, along with a few colleagues I conducted a search in his cell. I remember distinctly there was an India-Pakistan cricket match that day and all the prisoners were engrossed in it. Taking advantage of the fact that his cell was empty, we did a search and found smack hidden under his pillow. He had filed the case against me, but actually it was him who was dealing in smack inside Tihar! However, I realized that reporting it would be futile because the rules clearly say that unless you take along witnesses who search you to confirm that you carried no drugs with you to plant on the accused, the case falls flat. In jail, most recoveries of drugs are accidental. So if we went to look for some contraband in Grover's cell and accidentally stumbled upon his stash, he could turn around and say that I had planted drugs in his room as an act of vengeance to settle the complaint he had filed against me. The other problem was that the guards I took along with me would also not testify in court in support of my recovery. For the sake of a few grams of drugs, they were not going to upset their equation with whoever was Surender Grover's ally. So any judge, this case went to, would look at us with great suspicion.

However, that did not stop us fighting against such complaints. Drug abuse is perhaps the most rampant problem in jail and it impacts a large number of people. Desperation would make inmates come up with novel means of sneaking drugs in. Like once, a harmless-looking prisoner called Lala came to see me. He gave me a sob story about how he was diabetic and needed my permission to get the fruit, *jamun*. This fruit is meant to have qualities that help fight diabetes and so I allowed him to get some. Sometime later, guards from the Tamil Nadu police came to see me. They showed me the stash of 'medicinal' *jamuns* that Lala had procured. When one of them touched the *jamun*, it did not feel quite right. While the top layer was of the actual fruit, underneath there were plastic *jamuns* which were screwed together to hide the drugs in their cavity. This was not an isolated case. In my years at Tihar, I learnt that fruits are the preferred Trojan horse for drugs and other contraband. Finely-chopped bananas can hide currency notes and you can make *parathas* out of anything. Inside prison a packet of smack which normally costs Rs 100, can be sold for at least Rs 1,000. Besides, what is the worst that could happen? If you are caught, it is a police complaint that falls flat and if you get away with it, you are rich.

We tried hard to stop drug abuse in Tihar. I saw it as the biggest challenge to genuine reform and correction for the prisoners. In jail, at least there was some check on them, but when the same prisoners were released, they would ruin their families' lives as well as their own. And so, despite the fact that we had absolutely no teeth in drug-related cases, we still conducted raids and made life difficult for the peddlers. We wrote to the government and various law bodies asking for a change in the Narcotics Drugs and Psychotropic Substances Act of 1985 so that it did not ask for unreasonable provisions like the presence of a gazetted officer during a drug bust. Despite all this, drug related problems were widespread and continue to persist.

These, however, are problems of the poor and the ordinary. The rich find extraordinary means to gain comfort in jail. By now, thanks to the Chandra case or the V.K. Sasikala exploits, people know that you can buy a comfortable existence in prison. Sasikala, an aide to former Tamil Nadu Chief Minister J. Jayalalitha, was found to have a separate kitchen in a prison in Bengaluru where she has been since February 2017, doing time for gaining masses of wealth by questionable means. But all this seems passé when compared to

Manu Sharma, whose politician father bought a five-star hotel next to Tihar to supply him with food and cash for favours.

A brash 29-year-old Manu Sharma came to us in Tihar in 2006 after he was convicted for committing a murder. On 29 April 1999, Manu and his friends had gone to a party at the hip Tamarind Court Café in the Capital. At around 2 am when the bar had shut, he asked a model, Jessica Lall, who was the guest bartender for the night, and the bar owner and fashion designer Malini Ramani for a drink. They refused, saying the bar had shut. Sharma offered to pay Rs 1,000 in cash for a drink which Ramani refused once again. The management student replied, 'For a thousand rupees, I'll have a sip of you.'

It was at that point that Manu Sharma ensured his place in Delhi's crime hall-of-fame. Unable to deal with being refused a drink, he took out his Italian Berretta revolver and fired two rounds. The second shot hit Jessica in the head and she was declared dead on arrival at the hospital. The killing was instantaneous but Manu used his influence and a battery of lawyers to ensure that he did not go to jail until 2006. The lower courts acquitted him but the Delhi High Court bench under Justice R.S. Sodhi (the same one who was the lawyer in the Indira Gandhi assassination trial) retried the case and in December 2006, sentenced Manu to life imprisonment. While overturning the acquittal given by a lower court, Justice Sodhi said it was 'perverse' to let Manu Sharma walk free after shooting model Jessica Lall for refusing to give him a drink.

The judgement was extraordinary because of the clout that Manu Sharma's family wielded. His father Venod Sharma, a top Haryana Congress leader, was so powerful that scores of witnesses present at the party claimed to have not seen anything out of the ordinary the night of the shooting. Another model who was also bartending that night, Shayan Munshi, even claimed that the police statement he first gave nailing Manu Sharma was not genuine because he did not understand Hindi despite having worked in Hindi movies. There were top police officers, and even a Hollywood actor, Steven Seagal present that night, but the very expensive defence of Ram Jethmalani ensured that no one saw anything and Manu Sharma was acquitted. But in December 2006, the higher court stepped in and convicted Manu and his cousin, Vikas Yadav, the son of politician D.P. Yadav, for murder and destruction of evidence. The court found that Vikas had aided Manu by driving his car away from the scene of the crime and hiding it. There was nothing their families could do to save them from jail now.

From freedom, Manu Sharma went straight to facing his entire life in prison. I think for a long time the Sharmas felt that the Supreme Court would overturn the conviction. But in April 2010, the Supreme Court upheld the high court's decision ensuring that Manu Sharma and Vikas Yadav were sent to prison for a very long time. One of the first things their family did was to buy the Hilton Hotel only four kilometres from Tihar. They later renamed the hotel Piccadily and this proved to be highly beneficial for the Sharma family – not only did Manu have access to comfort but the quid pro quo system also became visible for jail staffers. Usually, there is an elaborate system that is set up for prisoners to secretly pay off their jailers, but in this case they could be wined and dined nearby. Starting 2006, the superintendent, deputy superintendent and many others in Tihar became a part of the 'Sharma payroll'. So much so that it was Manu who was considered the superintendent of Jail number 2. After 2010, and the acquisition of the hotel, his sphere of influence increased and he even secured jobs for their families at the hotel. A TV crew found that Neeraj Sharma, the son of P.C. Sharma, the additional superintendent of Tihar, had been working at the hotel in 2011 – he had also worked in the Sharma's original parent company.

If I was to do a conservative estimate, it would be fair to say that Manu got jobs for at least 50 relatives of jail staffers at the hotel. If the hotel could not use their services because they were overqualified, they would be accommodated at his brother Kartikeya's media company, News X. What's more, if a jail staff member had a wedding in the family, Manu's hotel was open to them. If food had to be ordered it would come from the hotel. I clearly remember Manu sitting with Director General Alok Verma and Inspector General Mukesh Prasad in their room and ordering food from there. He literally had the entire jail hierarchy eating out of his hands. This eventually led to the scathing report by the National Human Rights Commission (NHRC) who made a surprise visit in 2015 and found Manu enjoying unprecedented freedom to move around in jail and having the comforts of home in his cell – so much so that his cell looked more like a studio apartment and not a prison cell. For a while, after the report was published, Alok Verma was in trouble. However, everything has a fix and the bosses were able to somehow convince everyone that this was not a matter worth pursuing.

I admit that I went to Piccadilly too, for some family event post retirement in 2016. When the hotel staff got to know that I had served in Tihar, they were very nice to me. They offered me tea and coffee and showed me around the very fancy hotel. And I was impressed. The thing about Manu is that he paid bribes discreetly and did not act high handed and throw it in your face. In fact, if an officer came into the room, he would stand up like everyone else. Everybody in jail went to him whenever they needed help and he would somehow get the job done. For instance, there was a particularly tragic case where a man was imprisoned for murdering his wife, leaving their young children with no one to care for them. The judge asked me to admit them to a school or a care home in Rohtak, where they were from. I approached Manu Sharma because I knew he had good contacts in Haryana, thanks to his father. He took care of it immediately and even committed to pay for their entire education. He has an NGO under his real name, the Siddharth Vashishta Charitable Foundation that focuses primarily on looking after the children of prisoners.

Manu's influence did not just stem from money. He was connected to a lot of famous and powerful people and they all came to visit him in jail. Apart from his father Venod Sharma, many politicians dropped in to see him. These meetings would not take place in the usual *mulaqat* room but in the *deodi* or the reception area of the jail, right next to the top officials' offices. India's only individual two-time Olympic medallist Sushil Kumar, was a close friend of Manu's and visited him many times. In fact, because of this friendship, Sushil Kumar agreed to be the chief guest at one of our Tihar sports tournament.

I would not be exaggerating when I say that Manu Sharma single-handedly turned around TJ's, a brand under which products manufactured by Tihar prisoners is sold. He converted it from a Rs 6 crore business in 2006 to a Rs 31 crore business in 2016, the year I left Tihar. In ten years, Manu made a complete success out of TJ's that produces bakery items, handloom and textiles, furniture, oil, recycled paper and a variety of other products. Since every prisoner has to do some daily work, Manu put his management training to good use and harness this work force. It was he who suggested we open TJ's outlets in various places such as district courts. I thought the way he explained the efficacy of the project was brilliant. He said that if judges consume products that have been made by inmates, it will invariably spread a positive image of Tihar. He hoped they would be more compassionate towards prisoners if they ate something produced in Tihar and loved it. Basically, the effort was to humanize the inmates. To make the business grow, Manu also wrote letters to various companies, asking them to partner with us as a part of their Corporate Social Responsibility (CSR). And finally, he also suggested opening a restaurant within Tihar for outsiders. This was implemented too, and for a while it did really well. Perhaps thanks to those who believed in the superstition of eating jail food!

It was a combination of such facts that made Manu popular in Tihar – both amongst the staffers and the prisoners. I know how odd that sounds – how can a man who had done something so dreadful, be so popular; but you have to appreciate that jailers have a different sense of people. As an individual, I hated the idea of him, someone that could just kill a woman because she dared to refuse him a drink. But my years of experience in this occupation made me see him from a different perspective, and I could see beyond his crime. We do not hate the person but the crime they commit and our job was to treat them as humanely as possible so they had a chance of reforming. This is why I was not comfortable with what happened in the Nirbhaya case. Ram Singh's safety and well being was important to me, but he was denied security. In Manu's case, I was impressed by his efforts to reform himself by using his time in Tihar positively. In a place where everyone is a hardened criminal, it is not difficult for those who have kindness and behave themselves to stand out.

Sanjeev Nanda, the man behind the infamous hit and run BMW homicide, was another such prisoner who stood out. Being the grandson of a former Navy chief and the son of a wealthy arms dealer, Nanda was privileged, rich and had access to power. However, he did not flaunt any of these when he came to us. He was 22-years old when he came to Tihar but showed a maturity beyond his years. His family had paid off the relevant officer to ensure that he was comfortable and had a secluded space away from the underbelly of the jail. But by and large he followed the rules. He taught other inmates under a programme we had initiated called *Padho Padhao* (Study and Teach) for adult literacy. He was an enthusiastic teacher and taught English and computers to fellow prisoners. Nanda did not indulge in what we called *khula khel farukhbabadi* in Uttar Pradesh, which basically means that you openly break every rule in the book and don't make any pretence about it.

In complete contrast, Manu Sharma's partner in crime, Vikas Yadav, displayed brazen, deplorable behaviour even inside prison. While awaiting trial in the Jessica Lall case, Vikas had gone on to commit a murder of his own. Along with his cousin, Vishal, he murdered his sister's boyfriend Nitish Katara on 17 February 2002 because he did not approve of their relationship. Vikas was such a piece of work that nobody wanted to associate with him inside Tihar. Initially, he and Vishal were in the same jail as Manu Sharma which is Jail number 2 but they all wanted to be away from Vikas, so he was moved to Jail number 4 and Vishal to Jail number 1.

Manu often said that Jessica's murder was not his fault, but it was the company that he kept which was to blame. I don't know how that could be true but it said a lot when even your cousin did not want to be associated with you. Manu was quiet and sober while Vikas was a bully. He behaved badly with everyone and people were scared of him because he had nothing to lose – he was already connected to two murder cases. He roamed around freely in jail and no one really wanted to take him on.

In one instance I remember, Vikas Yadav checked into the All India Institute of Medical Sciences (AIIMS) on some pretext of treatment. When the nurse came to check him in the morning, the escort security of Delhi Police guards stopped her and said that she should not disturb his sleep. When she insisted and fought her way into the room, she found that Vikas had not even spent the night at AIIMS. He had left to spend Diwali in Uttar Pradesh with his family. Both the Delhi police and certain AIIMS staff had played a part in his escape. When the young nurse reported this, unsurprisingly, she was threatened. On another occasion, Judge Brajesh Garg came for a surprise check to Tihar and found Vikas Yadav roaming around freely. Judge Garg drew up a report on all that he had seen and submitted it to court. What is surprising, however, is that when newspapers reported on Judge Garg's report, they mentioned politician Suresh Kalmadi (in Tihar for corruption charges related to the 2010 Commonwealth Games) having tea with jail officials, but not a word about Vikas.

In comparison, Manu Sharma was very well behaved and when his name came up for recommendation for furlough, I supported it. The furlough system rewards good behaviour and has been recommended by various judges and law commissions. If for three years, you follow all the jail rules, you get an annual holiday of seven weeks, broken up in three instalments, one of three weeks and two of two weeks each. But Manu's popularity did not win him any favours with the director general at the time, Neeraj Kumar, who would always deny his furlough applications. I even argued in favour of Manu and asked the director general to take cognizance of his good behaviour and to see it as a privilege that he had earned. But it was not until Kumar's successor Vimla Mehra took over that Manu was allowed a furlough.

It should be pointed out here that very few prisoners would actually avail of the furlough. A majority of them were really poor so they had no concept of taking a holiday. They preferred staying in jail where they were guaranteed three meals a day. In fact, the poor did not avail of other rewards in jail either. To qualify for a semi-open jail an inmate needed 12 years of excellent conduct. Because of this cut-off, the ones who qualified were those who were sentenced to life-imprisonment and therefore mostly murderers. As an open jail inmate, you could work anywhere in the jail – as a gardener or at the TJ's outlet. And if you acted responsibly during this period of limited freedom, then you hit the real jackpot – being allowed to leave Tihar for the day and return at 8 pm. During Director General Alok Verma's tenure and shortly after I retired, Manu Sharma qualified for this open jail privilege. I am told every morning he would leave for his family firm's head office in Nehru Place, New Delhi and spend the day there. His brother who runs news channel, News X also sits in that office and I'm told that Manu helps out in the business now. I suppose this system is the maximum freedom that you can get as a convict, but barely 20 out of several thousand inmates have this benefit.

Today Manu is fighting with the Delhi government's sentence review board for an early release. After 14 years in jail, there is a precedent for life sentence convicts to be released. However, ever since Rajiv Gandhi's killers petitioned for an early release and Rahul Gandhi raised an objection, it has not been easy for people like Manu to get released earlier from prison.

~

After 35 years, I thought I had seen everything but the best was saved for the end. If my career here began with and was due to my encounter with Charles Sobhraj, it ended with billionaire industrialist Subrata Roy of Sahara. In March 2014, the Supreme Court sent him to Tihar because of his inability to pay back his investors a sum of Rs 39,000 crore. So the flamboyant 66-year-old businessman who used to party with the likes of movie stars Amitabh Bachchan, Anil Ambani and Aishwarya Rai, became a Tihar inmate and the market regulator, Securities and Exchange Board of India (SEBI), said he could not get bail until he raised the money he owed. But Subrata Roy's lawyers convinced the court that he needed to continue to do business in order to raise this amount.

For regulated periods, the court allowed the conference room of Tihar to serve as Subrata Roy's cell, which meant he became the only inmate in the history of Indian jails to have an air-conditioned stay. He also got internet and Wi-Fi access to hold video conference meetings and use cellphones and laptops. His staff of stenographers and assistants were allowed to stay from 6 am right through to 8 pm. And for this, the Supreme Court asked him to pay Rs 1.23 crores as charges to Tihar authorities. This privilege was only meant for a 57-day period stipulated by the court so that he could negotiate the sale of his luxury properties, but Subrata Roy got a red-carpet treatment for his entire stay of almost two years.

Forget bottled water and restaurant food, alcohol was now flowing freely in that specially created 'court complex'. In the past inmates had managed to sneak in a drink or two, but here in the garb of 'business' meetings, whisky was permissible. The secretarial staff allowance made by the Supreme Court meant that women were freely able to visit the VIPs (two Sahara executives were also imprisoned with Roy) in the conference room too. It was so brazen that not just the warder, even top officers like Director General Alok Verma, had to be in on it too.

Something about all this really upset me. Maybe it was the realization that no one listened to me anymore. It was 2015 and I was close to retirement and so when I would stumble into the bosses' room and find them eating with Manu Sharma or the Sahara chief, they would shut the door on me. I wanted to do something about it.

I decided to go meet the new chief minister of Delhi, Arvind Kejriwal. Administratively, we all reported to the Delhi Government and anti-corruption had been the chief minister's main plank. If anyone had the guts to take on Subrata Roy, it had to be the Aam Aadmi Party chief. The meeting was organized by the AAP standing counsel in Delhi High Court, Rahul Mehra. We knew each other due to my court appearances and I gave him a brief about why I wanted this appointment. It didn't take long before Rahul and I were sitting before the chief minister in April 2015.

This was going to be my last fight in Tihar. I told him about everything that I saw – how the jail system was being subverted because of gross bribery and corruption. For an hour, Arvind Kejriwal patiently listened to me and then asked me to come and meet him at his home after two days. Once again, Rahul Mehra helped me get an appointment and I coordinated with his assistant, Vaibhav, who finally summoned me to the chief minister's residence in June. This time, there were more people present at the meeting, including the Minister In-Charge of Prisons, Satyendra Jain who confirmed that he had also received complaints against Alok Verma for favouring certain prisoners. For his benefit, I reiterated what I had witnessed in the Sahara saga. As they served tea, I asked them to conduct a raid in Tihar so that all that I had alleged could be proved.

'Sunil, I know everything,' said Arvind Kejriwal, 'I need evidence. Get me a photograph or a video that can be shown. Otherwise, it's just another story.'

'I can't take a picture or a video,' I told him, 'But I can prove that Subrata Roy is being favoured.'

Kejriwal then turned to Satyendra Jain to ask him if a raid was possible. He nodded. I said, 'If you raid the jail in the evening you will even find alcohol bottles.'

'But who will get the blame for it?' asked Kejriwal. 'Won't it be the superintendent?' He was right. The entire blame would just be pinned on this one person and others would continue as if nothing happened. I mean, how do you capture things like senior officials touching Subrata Roy's feet, which I had seen with my own eyes. They were literally so servile in front of him. I told the chief minister that it was his decision. Maybe, I suggested, the raid could be followed up with an inquiry which would reach the top level of the director general. They said they would think about it and revert. I told them that the only reason I reached out to them was because I trusted them and respected their integrity. They thanked me and I left.

I did not hear from the chief minister or his colleagues for some time. I would bump into them at places and they would reiterate their intention and again ask to go for the big fish. 'We need to catch Alok Verma red handed,' was their message to me and I would always say that it was up to them, it was only my duty to inform them.

It was a month later in July that Alok Verma called me to his office.

'How do you know Satyendra Jain?' he asked, 'He praises you a lot.'

I told him that he was my local MLA and because he was the jail minister, I would meet him for official reasons. By now I was a bit nervous. The next day, I was called to Alok Verma's office again. This time, he made me wait for some time. When I went in, I noticed a distinct change in his behaviour.

'What is the need to go and meet political leaders? Don't you know this is against the rules of conduct?'

I was shocked when he added, 'You are the reason for the poor guy's loss.' It took me a while to realize that by 'poor guy' he meant Subrata Roy and the potential threat to his special facilities. His words to me were an overt signal that my complaint had fallen on deaf ears. I would have let it go but I learnt a few days later that they were planning to get back at me with some concocted charges and so I sought an appointment with Jain who assured me that I was being paranoid. Nothing would happen to me.

But it did. Just a week before I was to retire, I was handed a charge sheet stating that I had not settled the department's bills of around Rs 2 lakhs for a projector, screen and a laptop with fax machine. We were in July 2016 and the bills dated back from 2007–2014. I was outraged because these items were ordered by then two DGs: B.K. Gupta who ordered the screen and projector and Neeraj Kumar who ordered the laptop and fax machine. They had failed to clear the bills. Just because I had dared to raise an objection against the special treatment being given to Subrata Roy, they were trying to implicate me. And with what? It was basically a charge that I had not been able to get payments cleared during my tenure. How was it my fault, if the head of the prison, at the time, had not cleared the bills?

Through this Verma was able to make a whole complaint against me. They didn't even make the case details or the files available because had they done so, the government would clearly see that the bills had to be signed by the DGP and not me. The current DGP Alok Verma had refused to sign the bills because it happened before his time – it was a classic red tape ploy to harass me. There was nothing to the charges and yet, they had found a loophole with which to come after me.

A year later the bills were sent to Ministry of Home Affairs, where they were settled. But by then it was too late. They had managed to get their revenge. At the end of my term, after 35 years of service, I was robbed off the respect that I deserved. Even my staff took their cue from Alok Verma and hardly paid any attention to me. I would be sitting in office and the guards would be off somewhere else. Even my peon would find some pretext to not work. After all, who cares to listen to an out of favour jailer who is about to retire? The bitterness I had avoided my entire career, seemed to envelop me as a farewell gift. I was finally done with Tihar.

EPILOGUE

I have spent 35 years of my career in a prison, which if you think about it, is equivalent to serving two-and-a-half life sentences! My astrologer believes that in every hand there is a line that indicates if a person will go to jail – I had that too. Just not as an inmate.

It's been almost three years now since I retired as the law officer and do you know what I love about retirement the most? It's the luxury of not being imprisoned by routine. For all my working life, I had to wake up at six to get to Tihar on time, to make sure that there had been no unfortunate incident, that no one had run away and no one had been killed or injured.

Today, I still wake up early, by seven on most mornings, but now the only place I have to get to is my jogging park by 9 am. I stay there for the next couple of hours and only head out to my new job at midday. That's right, I am now a practising advocate of the Delhi High Court. In some ways my work is still related to prisons as I am the consultant for the National Legal Services Authority of India (NALSA) and organizations like the National Human Rights Commission (NHRC) keep inviting me to talk about prison reform. But I am no longer held accountable for what happens inside Tihar. Earlier, reporters would call me at all kinds of hours to demand answers. Now, I just leave the court at 6 pm and my work is done. It's a nice easy-going life and of all people, my wife, Poonam is the happiest that I'm done with my jail duty.

My prison career had made me tough, afforded me the strength to fight the corrupt – almost recklessly so, if I were to take on a gangster on my own to put an innocent person out of harm's way, I wouldn't shy away despite being forewarned. Naturally, Poonam was always worried. My adamant righteousness did nothing but feed the family's insecurities about my profession and it wasn't like I wasn't aware of that.

Things are better now. I have been spending all of my abundant spare time with the family, so we communicate more, understand each other better.

Reporters still call me though, but now I'm more of a talking head on TV, someone who can throw some light on the bizarre headlines that keep emerging from my former workplace. 'Smuggled mobile phones ring in trouble in Tihar', 'Prisoner swallows four mobile phones' are just some of the headlines that have appeared in the last few weeks. The TV studios all call me to ask, how does all this happen?

And that's the reason I decided to write this book. Till now, Tihar, or any other jail in India, has managed to keep its operations a secret. It's literally a block with no windows. Nothing comes out of there and the outside world has no idea how it, and other jails in the country, function. I was part of that world – where poverty and unemployment drives most of these people to crime and inside this block; where money trumps morality every time, no matter the criminals' class. But it's so closed that it would be impossible for me to now dig out even basic details like which superintendent is favouring which high-profile inmate. So I thought that it was time to demystify it, to let the world know the reality of our prison system so that someone would fix it.

I'm trying other methods too, to bring about reform. In a strange coincidence, on the day I retired, the Delhi High Court appointed me along with two other judicial officers as an inspecting official for jails. This would have meant that I would be the court's chosen person to independently verify if a prison was running according to rules, if all basic rights were being adhered to. I would have to visit the jail along with the other two appointees once a month and my connection with Tihar or any other jail, would continue. It didn't, however, work out because one of the other two officers got a promotion as a High Court judge. The other appointee couldn't really be bothered. In the end, I didn't push it because I wouldn't have minced my words and that would have meant more trouble coming my way.

But then as a lawyer, I do get to handle some significant cases for prisoner rights. I can proudly say that it was my petition that led to women getting the benefit of the 'Open Prison' system. This system, initiated in Delhi and many other jails across the country, incentivises good behaviour by letting those who have completed certain number of years live in a semi-open or an open jail. Semi-open jails are basically when the inmate is no longer in a cell all day, but is allowed to work around the jail, as a gardener, a cook, or any other job. If inmates spend time doing this for a couple of years without any violation, they then become eligible to be an open jail inmate, by which time they can actually leave the jail complex to pursue work outside and only have to come back at the end of the day. Thanks to our prodding, women prisoners can now get this benefit as well.

I am also the amicus curae (friend of the court) in the Delhi High Court case pertaining to those women prisoners who have mental health issues and face rejection from their families. We have been successful in the Social Welfare department opening halfway homes at six locations in the Capital with medical facilities. We're expecting final orders in the case which, I hope, will pave the way for landmark directions about women prisoners and their well-being.

I have got the ability to fight all these cases from my years at Tihar so if you ask me if I have any regrets, I really have none. It's the job which helped me raise my two children. Today, my daughter is married and my son has got a good job. So, I am happy to say, Poonam is no longer angry with me about my work in Tihar, she's much more relaxed. My work has also made me quite famous. Any article, any news report about Tihar would always include my name.

And I have some great stories to tell. Like that time when Kiran Bedi joined the prison department. She was this glamorous officer we only ever saw on TV or in the papers and then one day she walked into the prison to applause from the prisoners who saw her as the crusader for their rights. Or, all those times that Charles Sobhraj came to the inmates' and my aid in legal matters, deftly drafting petitions and appeals – no one could escape that charm.

Looking back, the only regret I have is the way I was treated in my last year of work. I couldn't take the way Subrata Roy was getting away with all these facilities and so I tried to speak up, but no one cared to listen. That's what happens when you near retirement. All those who used to be scared of you, they no longer care. And for taking it to the Delhi chief minister, they tried to initiate some inquiries against me. In April this year, retired IAS officer N. Balachandran concluded the inquiry initiated by Alok Verma against me with the words, 'From what has transpired at this inquiry, it appears there is an apparent bias against the CO (Gupta),' he wrote. Alok Verma had some troubles and inquiries of his own during his retirement this year. Just less than a month before his retirement date, he was shunted to the Fire Department from the prestigious post of CBI director in January 2019.

So, at the end of it all, would I have been happy if my son or daughter wanted to be a prison officer? Honestly, no. Yes, I came out of it fine and, yes, I am financially stable and have a unique skillset that makes me sought after today, but I don't think my children can handle it. I was able to survive with my integrity intact, but I don't think I want my children to go through all that. I think that my entire family has been through enough.

www.ingramcontent.com/pod-product-compliance
Lightning Source LLC
LaVergne TN
LVHW031431170726
843492LV00010B/2949

* 9 7 8 8 1 9 4 2 0 6 8 5 9 *